The Alchemy of Being a House

a memoir
about the Body that broke,
the Voice that barked, and
the Home that became us

Jen Peer Rich

Praise for
The Alchemy of Being a House

Jen Peer Rich is a natural born storyteller and writer. Her deeply heartfelt memoir deftly takes the reader on a journey into the troubled waters of addiction, trauma and loss. Jen's life has been an odyssey that some might not have had the strength to survive. The unwavering doggedness it took to heal, along with the magical relationship she cultivated with nature, taught Jen how to alchemize deep suffering into blessings. A bright light shines on this enchanting memoir showing us the power and strength of the human spirit.

— *Debra Rosenman, author of the multi-award-winning book, The Chimpanzee Chronicles: Stories of Heartbreak and Hope from Behind the Bars; Founder of Sacred Sorrowing.*

Circle of Selves Press™
www.jenpeerrich.com

This is a memoir, based on lived experiences, shaped by memories, and offered with care. Some names and identifying details have been changed to preserve privacy. Every person in these pages existed in my life, though their presence is filtered through time and my own healing lens. The stories are told as I remember them, with attention to emotional truth and respect for personal dignity.

Please note: this book is not meant to serve as medical, legal, spiritual, or psychological advice. I've shared my experience with honesty and depth, but my journey is my own. If you're navigating personal decisions related to health or wellbeing, please consult a trusted friend or professional.

Every effort has been made to present this book with integrity, but I cannot guarantee that all the information will be applicable to every reader or situation. No responsibility is assumed for any outcomes related to how the content is interpreted or used.

I'm not offering prescriptions, only presence. May this book accompany you, not instruct you. No one holds the blueprint of your becoming.

*The Alchemy of Being a House: A Memoir About the Body That Broke,
the Voice That Barked, and the Home That Became Us*

ISBN (Paperback): 979-8-218-70853-5
ISBN (Hardcover): 979-8-218-70854-2
ISBN (eBook): 979-8-218-70855-9

Library of Congress Control Number: 2025912335

First Edition, September 2025

Distributed worldwide

Interior formatting, layout and cover design by David Provolo

Editing by Michelle Ireland

Circle of Selves logo and The Alchemy of Being a House sigil by Jen Peer Rich

Table of Contents

Welcome To Our
Circle of Selves

The Circle of Selves is a three-part memoir series exploring healing, inner multiplicity, and the radical act of letting every part belong. Each book explores distinct, interconnected stories of survival, transformation, and selves-in-relationship. You'll meet my loyal inner watchdog, my fierce infant self, and the personified parts that make up our Body Voices. Together, they form a living map of what it means to come home to many selves, piece by piece, part by part. This sigil holds the heart of our trilogy. Each shape speaks. Each carries wisdom. Each holds a key.

Symbols:

Our Dog
Loyal. Vigilant. Wounded. Wise.
She is Ruth, the voice that barked when no one listened.
That held us when no one else could.
The one who guarded the threshold of our every transformation.
She's instinct, embodied.

Our Baby

Raw. Feral. Totally badass.

Baby Jenny spoke in our first language: rage.

Born speaking a native tongue the world couldn't decode.

Too much. Too loud. Too intense.

Too wild. Too alive.

She's our pulse, our sheer will to survive.

She doesn't scream, she howls.

Somehow, impossibly, she made it.

My avatar of infant survival, still burning bright.

Our Heart

Unfiltered truth. Gentle strength.

The living center of all our selves.

This is home.

The wild place where life is happening, memories pulse and healing is always in season.

Our Music

Echoes of each self's voice, sometimes clashing, sometimes clanging, sometimes harmonizing.

Each note is a part of our house, a sacred sound.

Together they form the music of our strange and beautiful inner world.

Our Circle

A shape that says:

You belong. You've always belonged.

Before You Come Inside

Can I share a few things first?

This is a memoir told from many angles. It arises through memories, family interviews, stories and pictures—years of autoethnography research. Names and identifying details have been changed in some instances to protect privacy.

The first part of each chapter is narrated by me, Jen—set during the winter of 2022, as I moved through a season of caregiving, uncovering secrets, memories, and miracles. The second part of each chapter is narrated by Ruth—my inner voice, a dog, my guardian, the vigilant part of me forged in the trauma I experienced as a baby. Ruth's sections move back in time. She remembers what I can't. Sees what I don't see. Goes where I don't go.

Ruth isn't a metaphor. She's real, just not in a way most folks are used to. When Ruth speaks within the sections of the book, you'll find her in *italics*. When she takes the mic in full, her sections are clearly labeled: **Ruth**. You'll know by the shift in time, space, and rhythm. This is how Ruth and I remember our life, together.

Between some chapters you'll find something different, something more. These spaces belong to Ruth, it's where you'll find her wisdom unleashed. Think of these points as windows that open inward and let some fresh air into our house.

This book is about truth-telling from my point of view and interpretations. I've done my best to tell it with tenderness, even when it is hard. My intention is not to blame or shame, but to unearth the buried parts of myself, so that others might feel less alone in theirs. My family survived things that shaped us in different ways. We each have our own stories. This is my part of our story, with all its guts, grit, and grace.

To support your journey through *The Alchemy of Being a House* I've created a free digital welcome kit, a set of house keys for tired bodies, sensitive hearts, and curious minds.

Inside you'll find:

• An invitation to begin softly

• A gentle guide to reading at your own pace

• An introduction to Ruth and her voice as my inner guard dog. She showed up when I was a baby to keep me safe and never really left.

• Free resources: bookmarks, voice notes, audio reflections, and more invitations to come

Everything is optional. Everything is offered with love, no strings attached. Take what you need. Leave what you don't.

Pick up the keys at: www.JenPeerRich.com

Blueprints for a Living House

We are a house made of houses. Each one layered inside the next, rooms within rooms, lives within lives. Some of us fell apart in one. Others rebuilt in another. There are parts still learning how to live inside the scaffolding of old selves healing, and new selves still forming.

Each house has its own time, its own rhythm. Some hold the echo of slammed doors. Others, the hush of steady reclamation. All of them are still breathing. All of them are ours. We are a living house.

This home, the one we share, remakes itself moment to moment. It threads together with witnessing. With presence. With the quiet courage it takes to stay, to not run away from our parts.

It heals a little more every time someone arrives, opens a door, and sees what's inside. Walk slowly. Breathe. Take breaks when you need to. If you get lost, look for Ruth, she never forgets the way home.

The Way In

Everyone starts as a house.

It's the staying, softening, and tending
that makes a house a home.

Threshold

Some people are born into life. I was flung into mine.
A car crash when I was a baby cracked open the terrible
truth of a hidden tumor.
Years later, another trauma cracked me open, this time into
a kind of unconventional motherhood no one saw coming.

My daughter, born of betrayal,
undeniably wrapped in an otherworldly magic.
The fierce and holy guru that wrecked me,
and remade me, over and over again.

Love didn't come in safe packages.
It wore the wrong uniforms.
Healing showed up like a disaster in drag.
Transformation rarely arrived through best-laid plans—
mostly through rupture.
Through breakdowns that became portals.
Unravelings that stripped away everything that wasn't mine,
that wasn't true, so I could remember how vast I am.

Some call it synchronicity.
I do too.
But not in the love-and-light, bypass-the-hard-shit kinda way.

More like this: there's a seam where the invisible stitches
itself into the visible.
When I'm still enough, broken enough, naked enough,
something ancient rises up from within me.

It buzzes with the sound of old knowledge.
I call it alchemy.
That flicker of alignment between the universe's purpose
and our own.
The way that what was raw and untouchable for so long,
now rests within me with the weight of wisdom.
Not better.
Not fixed.
Just more true.
More integrated.
More aligned.

I used to think healing meant I could somehow erase the
wreckage of my life.
Now I know: healing makes the wreckage holy.
It turns scars into stories,
stories into maps,
and the map into a home.

One room inside me is fashioned entirely of pain.
Bone and metal grinding.
Walls painted with heavy coats of scar tissue and sheer will.
It creaks, swells, groans, and expands with weather.

My spine is fused from my neck to my pelvis.
My body, well worn by pain and disability, is full of life.
I don't live in a body that moves easily.
But it's the kind of body that stays.
Adapts.
Plays.
Clings on for dear life.

Wise beasts live in me.
Some parts are protectors.
Others are soft children.
Time travelers and wild-eyed mystics.
I am possums and dragonflies.
One self is a dog.

Yep, a dog.
Her name is Ruth.
She's hypervigilantAF.
Hypervigilance gets a bad rap.
But it's just love with extra sensors.
She's Loyal.
Fierce.
The one who stayed with me when no one else did.
Touched me when no one else could.
The one who never slept when danger was near.
She guarded doors I wasn't ready to open.

She's traveled with me through every story.
Sat at every threshold and waited,
even when I locked myself out of my own body.
Tracked me through mazes and detours.
Watched the perimeter when I could barely function.
She was there in the fog.
In the fury.
In our long forgetting of each other.
And still, she stayed.
This is her story too.
Ours.

The turning point didn't come with a lot of noise,
although it did make the noise a lot more clear.
Healing arrived in the quiet.
Under a canopy of trees in my backyard.
Not fixing myself.
Just...BEing myself.

Tree roots, deep underground, they held me.
Inspired me.
Cheered me on through my dark night of the soul.
The breeze moved through the branches,
and kissed me right on my heart like a recognition.
A reminder.
A remembering.

Down there in the roots, soft voices whispered: you belong.
No need to prove anything.
To fix anything,
No need for acceptance.
Just the tacit awareness that I belong to this miracle of life.
Unqualified.

I had a breakdown that turned into a breakthrough.
It wasn't flashy.
There were no visions.
No easy answers.
It was just me.
Alone, but not really.
Bare, but covered with care.
I was one with the sunlight filtering through the leaves.
With the sense—the deep, cellular sense that I was inside of
something true.

That I was loved from the inside out.
Always loved.
It was an awakening.
One sparked by crisis,
that became a kind of communion.
It was a summer of slowly, softly returning home to myself,
again and again and again.
An ordinary being remembering our birthright of
belonging.

I remembered I'm not one fixed self.
I am a circle of selves.
A blueprint.
A living house.
Full of rooms.
Some lit with memory.
Others locked with secrets.
Quite a few are in mid-renovation.
Many stand proud.
I am a house of hallways going nowhere
and everywhere at once.

We were born in the wreckage.
Still, we're here.
Alive.
Reassembled.
Stitched together by scars and golden threads.
Full of love,
creativity and potential.
Unafraid of who I am.
Of who we are.
Who we've been.

I think we're ready to let you in now.
That belonging I reclaimed under the trees,
it didn't fade when summer passed.
It moved with me.
Into me,
as me,
within me.
Belonging isn't something I reach for anymore.
It's not something I need.
It's who I am.
What I am.
Belonging is the reality woven into the walls of our house,
not just the literal one I share with Iris, Frannie, and our
pups,
but the deeper one I carry inside.

A forever home in the world.
And a home, at last, within myself.

This is our story of survival.
It's not a confessional.
It's not an explanation.
It's a map of return.
The imprint of alchemical transformation.
This is the sound of a soul singing itself back to life.

Welcome to the alchemy of being a house.

Chapter 1:

Collapsing

Jen — Winter 2021

The phone rings. I answer before I'm fully awake. "Jen?" "Mama? Everything OK?"

I hazy-eye the clock: 6:18 AM. My phone stares back at me like an alien in the dark. I fumble for the lamp and flick it on, squinting against the light as I push on my glasses.

"No. Something's wrong. I called an ambulance. I need to go to the hospital."

"OK Mama, I'll be on my way there with Iris soo—" Click. She already hung up.

I stare at the phone in my hand. Try calling her back. No answer. I try again. Still nothing.

Thickness spreads across my chest, slow and sure, honey mixed with dread. If she's calling an ambulance, it's bad. She doesn't ask for help. She's the toughest bird I know, she only cries wolf when the wolves are real.

Ruth's pacing the hallway inside me. Tail high. Ears cocked. She's on high alert.

Get going. She needs us.

I listen to her. I always do when she paces like that. Instincts older than logic. Older than language really. I can't pull myself out of bed. My spine is lined with angry protesters holding signs, shouting grievances, for a general strike. They say these are unfair working conditions inside my body. I agree.

I call my wife, Iris, who answers on the second ring. She's working early at the airport.

"Babe, I need you to come home. Mama's on the way to the hospital."

"I'll be there soon as I can."

She doesn't ask for details. Just moves. That's who she is—swift, steady, the calm that cuts through the chaos and finds me wherever, whenever I'm unraveling.

I drop the phone into my lap and fold myself back under the blankets, like I can somehow rewind the moment. Maybe I'm still dreaming. None of this has landed yet. Not really. My bedroom holds its breath with me. The silence is loud. Constricted. A pressure cooker, not full of rice or oatmeal, but something heavier, my boiling reality.

I reach for my water bottle, take a sip, and swallow hard hoping it might anchor me back into my body. I'm a ghost hovering somewhere above myself. That's how it is when hypervigilance kicks in, it lifts me right up and out my body before I even know it.

Ruth's still pacing, ears pitched, body alert. A siren in dog form. Hallways inside me flicker. Doors slam shut. Doors fling open. I follow her cue, and pull myself to the edge of the bed as thoughts scatter like birds spooked from a wire. I can already tell today is gonna ask for more than I have to give.

Iris is coming. That thought clicks into place like a light in the dark.

"She's coming," I say out loud, just trying to tether myself to the sound of it.

Ruth snaps, *Mama won't want us at her house. Book a room.*

Right. Yes. I grab my phone and pull up the app to book a reservation. A two-room suite at a hotel in downtown Huntsville. I start making plans without a second thought.

Mama lives in Owens Cross Roads, Alabama. We live in Atlanta, three and a half hours away. I haven't stepped inside her house in years—that was her boundary, not mine. Ever since Lamar died, that's how it's been. We meet in neutral zones. Shopping plazas. Someplace for lunch. Garden centers. Quick hugs in parking lots. *"Love you super much, have a safe trip home,"* with a sideways squeeze. Mama never hugs from the front. She keeps her distance from everyone, including me. It's been that way as far back as I can remember.

People call her the Mean Marine, for good reason. She's pretty damn spicy! Always has been. She enlisted right out of high school when she turned 18, it was 1964. Mama didn't stay in the Marines, but the Marines stayed inside her, as she says, Semper Fi. She left the service to work with computers before computers were a thing. That's where she met Dad.

Then she went into logistics at an aerospace company, and many years later, met my step-dad, Lamar.

On the phone, me and Mama are pretty close. It's all funny GIFs and emojis, good morning and good night texts — **I love you super much.** But the minute, and I mean the very minute we share physical space, everything shifts. We're like magnets turned the wrong way, pulled towards each other by design, pushing against each other the second we touch.

What if she can't go home? What if she's too sick to care for the dogs? The house?

Ruth's already got all the tabs open in my brain. Running simulations. Making calculations that rival the most complex physics.

I finally pull my way out of bed and get to work. I start throwing things I think I'll need on the bed in a pile. Jeans. Layers. Long underwear. Thermals. Long socks. My red rain boots go by the door, smooth and rubbery, ready for Alabama icy damp. The kind of cold that seeps into the bones and keeps them frozen.

I grab a bag for the dogs and fill it with puppy pads for our two weenie boys. Wicky is blind and Pax is just stubborn, he hates to pee outside.

I find a bag for Frannie. She's thirty-four, but a real life time traveler—thirteen on some days, eight on others. Her face always carried sweet innocence, her words a faint lisp. Her clothes never obeyed the seasons: tank tops in winter, heavy hoodies in summer. Rain jackets on sunny days. She lives in her own weather system, often wild and changeable day to day.

She was shaped by the worst kind of early harm, total betrayal by her biological mom and dad. So much unresolved pain passed down to her fragile soul directly through her own bloodline. She was forged by a childhood marked by deep fractures. Developmental disabilities no one understood. Mental illness no one named with care. Before I adopted her, she'd already survived so much. Not just at the hands of her parents, but failed foster placements where she was abused again. She went from one nightmare to another. The kind of neglect that leaves invisible scars. She didn't have words for what she'd been through. She didn't need words, her body screamed it all. Her fear. Her fury. Her fierce will to survive.

She has a different bloodline, through adoption, but no less my blood. Just before she turned eighteen, she moved into a group home where she lived for over a decade. She needed that intense support, back then that sweet face could really surprise you with a swift hard kick in leg when she was pissed. Over the years she's mellowed out, the violent outbursts came less and less, until finally not at all.

In the group home she became dangerously overweight and over-medicated. Four years ago Iris and I asked her if she wanted to come and live with us permanently. She said yes. It's been messy, difficult, and nothing short of miraculous to help her thrive. Our lives run like clockwork, because that's what she needs: solid routines, soft corners, dependable connections. There've been many chapters in our lives together, but this is the best one yet. She'll always need a circle of care to help her find her way. We're lucky to be that, it's an honor to shape that circle for and with her.

"Frannie!" I snap busting into her room where she's

sleeping soundly. "Grandma's going to the hospital. We need to be with her, OK? ...OK!"

Her head lifts slowly, "OK, Mama, I'm gettin' up." Her words wobble with worry. She loves Grandma. Always has. There's a bonded thread woven between them that doesn't need explaining. It just is, thick, taut, and alive.

By the time Iris arrives home, I've pulled everything into haphazard piles. She sweeps in and turns it all into perfect order. Clothes into stacks. Bags into the trunk. Loose plans into real ones.

"I'm taking tomorrow off," she says.

I nod. "We'll have the weekend. Everything is going to be okay."

Ruth raises an eyebrow, *What makes you think that?*

I don't know. I don't know anything right now. Mama had surgery two weeks ago—hiatal hernia repair. Her intestines pushed up into her chest. I wanted to come help her. I asked if I could be there and help take care of her. She said in no uncertain terms, no. She was fine. Always fine. She insisted on being left alone ever since Lamar died.

Ruth's voice sharpens. *What if she doesn't make it?*

I freeze.

What if you can't get into the house?

I'll call a locksmith.

How will you live without her?

I don't know. I won't. That's the truth of it. I feel like I might die too. Mama and I are polar opposites wired with the same voltage. Always repelling, always snapping right back. Push-pull. Push-pull. Abrasive love twisted into our very own intractable knot.

We pile into our car, Frannie's up front in the passenger seat, headphones on, the tablet glow has all her attention. Iris always drives. She's brilliant with directions, logistics, and math. All the things I struggle with. Not just struggle, more like a soul gripping inability to stay inside the lines. I'm dyslexic. If you ask me for directions, and I say go right, definitely go left! My brain reverses the most ridiculous things. Being dyslexic means I see the shape of things way before I know the name of them. It's a kind of non-local awareness. My mind never plays by the rules. It cavorts. It leaps. It skips. It bounds. It breaks the rules of time and space, sometimes landing me somewhere much more interesting than logic ever could.

Frannie's at about a third or fourth grade level on paper, but her kind of wisdom isn't the kind that abides by levels. It comes in bright flashes like lightning. We never know when those are coming, but when they do, it lights up the whole space with spellbinding insight. Frannie and I have our own kinda smarts that work just fine for us.

I curl into the back with the dogs. Pillows stuffed around my spine like packing material to brace my broken body. It's a three-and-a-half-hour ride to Mama's house. Just a little further over the mountain to get to Huntsville, the city nearby. Every mile is memorized by heart. A corridor between past, present, and future versions of me. I lean my head against the window, watching trees blur past, bare-branched sentinels. Trees of every kind have stood witnesses to my healing—across the years, seasons, and landscapes.

We met in Huntsville, Iris and I. A meeting that was

actually a homecoming. Before her? That town broke me. I ran away with a young man in the military. I was sixteen years old. Came back twice divorced after I married another guy in the military. I was nineteen. Two failed marriages before I was twenty. I came back even more broken. With a kid I barely knew, or knew how to care for, but committed to with my whole soul. Frannie was wild. Full with rage, rightful for what she'd been through. The first time I laid eyes on her, she was six. I was nineteen. We tried to build our life on broken wings, but we couldn't fly because we were both loaded down with unbearable weight.

Ruth murmurs, *Don't forget to mention the hate.*

I didn't. I won't. How could I? Self-hate loaded like a gun cocked right towards myself. I didn't know how to care for myself, let alone Frannie. It's possible to commit to loving someone with your whole heart and have no idea how to take care of them. I thought I was destined to live like that, practically homeless on the inside. Trying to be a mom without a map or any sense of direction.

Huntsville held some of my worst mistakes as much as it held my deepest devotions. It's where I brought Frannie for help. I kept trying to stitch our life together from scraps. It's where Dad reappeared, then vanished again. Where Mama and Lamar kept saving me. Their love was so real. So necessary. I didn't know it then, but they were holding up the corners of my life while it collapsed inward, again and again. That town was where I started saving myself.

And where you started to be a friend on the inside. A friend to me.

Yah. Ruth and I learned the hard way to listen to each other.

The sign blurs past: Huntsville City Limits. We're here. It's late at night, everyone's on edge and tired. We check into our hotel, a time capsule of the '90s. Jewel-toned carpet, dulled brass fixtures. A little odd. Weirdly comforting.

Frannie flops onto one of the beds, logs into Wi-Fi and focuses on her tablet. Wicky pees on the pad. Pax barks until I lift him onto the bed, where he takes up his usual watch-tower on the pillows at the top.

Iris hands me a bag. "Masks are in here."

"God, I love you," I say. I mean it. Every cell.

I leave them to rest and I head to the hospital. Mama's still in the ER.

The lobby smells like overripe antiseptic and long waits. My body tightens. It remembers hospitals the way some people remember songs. It remembers cancer. IVs. Radiation. The tangy taste of metal on my tongue. Being a baby in a plastic box marked *Do Not Touch*.

I scan for trees outside the windows that line the rear of the hospital waiting room. I send down my roots. Call in my tree friends who always help me to ground, come back to the moment instead of getting spun around the carnival rides inside my mind.

Ruth hums, *Mask*.

I press it against my face, loop the plastic around my ears, and step up to the ER check-in. My feet ache so bad. My back is on fire from the car ride. I wanna fold right there, but I can't. Mama needs me.

They send me to Bay 14, my boots squeak loud against the floor drawing attention right to me. I nod at nurses, the janitor, their eyes are kind, but tired behind the masks.

I always made nurses laugh when I was a kid. Ever since Covid, smiles are gone at the hospital. That's its own kind of sadness.

I find Mama inside slumped over a tray, breath hitching in gasps. Her skin's the color of moon milk. She doesn't talk, just claws the wet washcloth tight against her neck with one hand.

"She's vomiting nonstop," the nurse says. "We're admitting her."

Mama's curled up on the gurney, one hand clutching a blue puke bag against her mouth, her whole body rolls with dry heaves. It sounds like something's ripping loose inside, but nothing comes up. Just hollow, gasping retches that suck the life force right out of her. It's an awful sound, the desperation of needing to empty something that isn't there. I stay with her until my body just can't hold upright anymore. "I'll be back, Mama," I whisper. "I love you." She doesn't respond, just waves a hand towards the door. She never says a word.

Outside, the night sky feels darker than its usual dark. Stars are blurred by clouds. It's almost midnight. New Year's Eve.

The next morning we leave Frannie at the hotel with the pups, a pile of snacks, and downloaded shows to create their own cozy little kingdom. Iris and I drive to Mama's house. The highway that used to be sleepy, now roars with traffic day and night. The cornfields are bare. Winter stripped everything, the entire landscape scraped clean like a page halfway through being erased.

We pull into her gravel driveway, that popping sound underneath the tires so familiar to me. My nervous system knows that sound like it knows hospitals. This place was once my home too. It used to be a happy place. Dreamscape

Gardens—Mama and Lamar's garden where they grew and sold the most beautiful daylilies, now is a tangle of frostbitten weeds. Metal arches sag. Cement statues have been consumed by vines. Crumbling pots sit stacked like offerings to a place that once used to be a shrine. A faded sign still hangs above the door to the garage, hoping someone will show up to buy some flowers. No one comes. No one's been around here in a long time.

The back door is unlocked. We step into the house to find a chorus of barking, six old dogs with cloudy eyes. Her pack. Her reason. Her church. Mama had a strict policy about any rescue dogs she adopted out: if it wasn't a good fit for any reason with their adoptive family, they would come back to Mama. These dogs were all returned for one reason or another.

The house is cold, the kind of cold that's not just about temperature. There is a vacancy in the air. Space heaters hum from scorched outlets. Burn marks crawl up the walls like dangerous little goblins, their feet leaving trails of soot warnings.

Music plays from another room—mournful, Old Time music. Familiar. Forgotten. Mama always has music playing in the house, the sound drowns out the noise of the busy highway outside. Drowns out the noise of Mama's mind. It helps her relax, she says.

There's tenderness too. Warm gold paint on the walls that she brushed on herself. Potted houseplants have tiny signs with names and detailed notes about them scribbled on paper tucked underneath. A beta fish, Hong Hua, circles in silence.

Make sure you feed the fish.

Mama loves plants. Animals. Even when she couldn't love us, or show it, anyway, she loved nature. When she was a little girl she would walk for hours in silence with her Dad, just to get away from her Mom who was prone to screaming fits.

Then the smell in Mama's house hits me. A hard slap of mildew, decay, and the sour tang of something very unwell. I spot buckets of bloody puke. Mold clinging to vents and corners. Spider webs. A literal hole in the floor, straight down to the dirt crawl space below— a slab of plywood tossed over it like maybe denial could double as a floor. The water heater's leaking. Faucets are leaking.

We tackle what we can. Do as much as we can do to clean, to make things right. We work all day, separately and together, in shocked silence. Silence that says everything and nothing all at once. Silence that wraps tight around my brain. Around my heart. We can't name yet what we're holding, but it's already understood.

We do what we can, which doesn't feel like anywhere close to enough. Which is to say, we begin, without knowing the next right move.

Ruth hums fervently: *This is bad. At least we're here.*

Iris and I make a list. Tuck the dogs in makeshift dens, layering on all the old towels and blankets we can find. We turn off the fire hazards and seal the house.

Driving back to the hotel, our silence continues, thick, clinging to our clothes, our breath, our skin. Frannie's managed to take care of herself, the hotel room, and the pups. I kiss her, tell her she's done great. She nods like I'm a nuisance, never taking her eyes off the iPad. It's been a lot, for all of us. Iris stands in the small kitchen eating peanut butter from a spoon. We're fraying at the edges of the unknown.

I shower, keeping the door cracked, in case I fall. In case my body decides it's had enough.

Then I'm back to the hospital again. I make my way through the maze, the fluorescent lights and endless thresholds. Outside, the trees wait—constant, still, like they always have. I feel the trees grounding me. So does Ruth.

Mask. ID.

I find Mama asleep in the dim room she's been assigned, tucked between beeping machines and blinking monitors. Her skin's fever-bright, waxy. Her breathing is shallow, measured, distant, like she's already half-gone. It seems like we're losing her. I sit on a reclining chair next to her, trying not to make anything worse with my presence. I fold my hands. Unfold them. Fold them again. Try to get back into my body by leaning into the smoothness of the vinyl chair.

"*Happy New Year, Mama,*" I whisper through my mask. Nothing.

Ruth settles beside me, unseen but so very present. Her weight anchors me in the chair, in the room, in the whole situation. She's familiar now, my own weighted blanket on the inside.

Mama's so sick.

Just like when you got sick? When I was born to you? Ruth asks, tilting her head downward.

No. Not like that. Let's hope not, anyway. But some stories live deep in the cracks of our foundation. And Ruth, she's the one who answers the door when the past comes knocking.

Ruth — 1974

*S*ome stories split you so wide open you can't climb out, you have to dig down first. Down into the dark. Down into where the foundation cracked and the pain set in deep. Only then can you come up through it. That's where I come in.

I've always been here. Teeth bared, but only when needed. Mostly circling our inner rooms, pacing the edges of every situation, every breach, every fault line. I know the boards that bend under pressure. I watched the walls learn to distrust. Tracked every betrayal that stitched itself into her skin. I'm the guardian in the floorboards of Jen's house. My duty as a watchdog never ends. I know where everything is buried, because I helped her bury it.

You don't find the bones by walking the brightly lit halls. You find them by crawling down into the belly of what broke. Into the darkness. The crawlspace. Let's go to the first house. The one that breathes under our skin all these years later.

Don't stray. This house is hard to come back to. But I can smell it, you're ready now. Let's go.

Christmas lights blink slow and tired over a wide gold-framed mirror, throwing weak colors into the corners of the room. Their reflection pools across a brown naugahyde couch, cheap plastic made to look like leather, it sighs like a sad baby whenever anyone sits. The furniture is ripe with the smell of stale cigarettes and the kind of regrets that settle deep into the cracks like lost change.

Below the hum of flickering lights, a balding middle aged man slumps low in a dirty white T-shirt and sagging briefs.

Dad. His eyes are glassy, as always. He's fishing through an empty Pall Mall pack like he might find heaven down there at the bottom. What he finds is a wet, bent cigarette. He lights it anyway.

The TV show *Guiding Light* is blaring. Dad lives for the soaps. In this episode, the leading man, Malcolm, lays dying in a hospital bed after a heart attack. He ends up there after an argument with Georgine, who accuses him of having an affair with Rita—an affair she only knows about after she secretly followed him to Springfield. Dad is a thousand percent engrossed in their scripted love triangle.

The show abruptly ends with dramatic music. Credits roll. A commercial comes on. A man in a crazy jacket is shouting about Denevi Camera:

"Your camera take lousy pictures? Flash broken? Doesn't work? Great! My friend Frankie will give ya twenty bucks for that camera, even if it's broken...right, Frankie? BUT you gotta buy this Minolta 450E pocket camera. It has built-in-flash, a close-up-lens, an electric-eye, and you're gonna take great pictures with it! Won't ya Frankie?!"

Frankie, a credible guy wearing a wide necktie and a beige leisure suit flashes up on the screen and replies, "I guarantee you'll save money!"—just as the melodic jingle rings out: *Dublin, Berkeley, San Lorenzo, Cupertino, San Jose...*

Dad raises his glass and gestures toward the TV like Frankie's an old friend sitting right there in our living room. "Cheers to that, Frankie!" He brings the glass to his lips only to find, like his pack of smokes, it's also empty. Frustration mounts.

His three year old son is proudly perched on a newly opened Christmas present: a motocross-style three-wheeled red trike with thick black vinyl rear wheels and a big #9 banner on the front. The trike is too big, but that doesn't get in the way of his delight. He pushes himself quietly around the living room, stretching to his tiptoes, paddling his feet with all his might rather than using the pedals. No matter what, Big Brother knows not to disturb Dad when the soaps are on.

Jen is six months old, asleep on the couch in a pillow fort next to Dad so she doesn't fall off. She sleeps a lot. When she's not sleeping, she's a fussy baby. Uninterested in suckling Mama's nipples. She doesn't care to eat much. Dad doesn't have patience to get her to take a bottle. She screams. She howls. Inconsolably.

The TV signal flickers in and out. Dad glances at the clock: 3:58 PM. "Damn. Fuck! Fuck."

His eyes lower, making out the shape of his baby daughter still sleeping beside him. He's late picking up Mama from work. Again. Between that, the empty pack of smokes, an empty glass, and the end of his soap, he decides it's time to take the couch party on the road.

He pulls his body to the edge of the seat cushion, arms straining to lift his own weight. His legs are two wet noodles. They don't respond. His eyes spin like marbles dropped down the drain. He's super drunk. A day of TV watching and cheap wine will do that to a person.

"Come on, we're gonna go pick up yer mom," he mutters.

He manages to stand with the support of the couch behind him. He catches sight of his pants on the floor and snags them with his toes, pulling them closer. Flailing in slapstick style, he struggles to aim his drunken legs into the small pant holes. It's a funny sight. Big Brother laughs with Dad and yells—"Clown-time!" A moment of levity in a home gripped by heartsickness.

Dad barrels himself upright, buttons and zips his pants,

then lifts Jen, now stirring from their laughter. Big Brother loves his dad, he instinctively grabs a back pocket rather than reaching for a hand. The back pockets match his height. The threesome make their way to the VW parked outside, Big Brother guiding his dad from behind like an old friend at the bar after a long night of drinking. Jen's too big for a one-armed carry, but too small to fight it.

They pile in, Dad plops Jen into the passenger seat. Her body slumps. Her diaper squishes. He wraps the seat belt around her twice, a makeshift restraint, then climbs behind the wheel.

The car reeks of booze. He coughs, revs the engine way too hard. "Hang on," he slurs. The radio screams songs in static. Big Brother babbles in the backseat. Jen's sock foot twitches in protest.

They never make it to pick up Mama.

Halfway there, the car veers off the road and slams into a guardrail. A slow-motion wreck. The gearshift slams hard into Jen's back. She rolls onto the floor of the car, screaming. Dad doesn't check on her. Or Big Brother in the backseat. He leans against the steering wheel, eyes wide, mouth slack. "Fuck."

Family lore differs after that.

Dad tells it like it was some holy accident. "They found the tumor because of me," he brags every chance he gets. "Because of the wreck. You're alive because I'm a drunk." His mouth is full of justifications. Like her survival somehow makes his behavior noble.

Mama tells it another way.

She took Jen to the hospital the next morning for a Well Baby appointment. "She wasn't right last night," she tells the nurse. "She was making...I don't know, weird sounds, not sleeping. I can tell she's hurting. Something's not right."

The nurse tracks the bruise on Jen's back from the gear-shift. Mama reads her silence. Her instant stiffness. Things move fast. X-rays. Medical jargon that sounds like a foreign language. Something on her spine. A shadow taking up the space of her entire abdomen where no shadow should be.

No longer in a crib or arms, Baby Jenny is placed inside a clear plastic box. A baby aquarium. Sterile and suffocating. She knows she doesn't belong there. She screams for help. Can't anyone hear her? She's too big for an incubator, but they put her in one anyway. She's labeled. Tagged. A baby boxed in under a sign reads:

DO NOT TOUCH.

Mama presses one hand against the plastic box and points firmly towards the sign. Her voice indignant, "Can't I hold her? Can't you see she needs to be picked up?"

"We're worried the tumor might rupture, she can't be held. It might've already ruptured. She can't be touched..."

And right here, dear reader, this is where I begin. This is my birth story.

That's where I, Ruth—the part of Jen forged in the absence of touch—take my first breath.

I'm the bark inside her chest. The guard at the gate. I'm the touch she didn't get. I'm the weight that steadied her. The pressure that said: I'm here. You're not alone. The one who never leaves. Baby Jenny couldn't be held. But I could hold her. And I did. And I do. I will. Forever.

My first job was wrapping around her like a second skin. Not seen, not named, just there.

A low hum. A willing growl. A watchful press. A breath that wasn't hers but always stayed close enough to borrow from.

This is how we begin.

Within hours, Baby Jenny is transferred, and we're really

lucky for that. Lucky to call California home, we lived a stone's throw away from Stanford University. A lifesaving place. The doctors don't say cancer yet, but it hovers in the air. Mama watches as the ambulance takes her baby away. She doesn't cry. Not there. Not yet. She doesn't have the privilege of falling apart.

She's got no car. No money. Dad's gone again. But she's got a whole lot of grit.

She climbs onto the city bus with a paper sack of hope clutched to her chest. Transfers to another line, and walks the last block to the bank. Every step lands as both a worry and a prayer. Every breath is a quiet plea for something. Some kind of break.

She sits in the bank lobby with a trembling kind of determination. Everyone there knows Dad, knows what he did. That's what Mama thinks, anyway. The purse in her lap is proud, like Mama. Her red curly hair is wild and worn, stubborn as ever. Her heart's a radio still tuned to the station that was playing when Dad wrecked the car. The stuffy air takes up all the space as she waits.

A door opens, and out walks a woman who looks like she's stepped straight out of a J.C. Penny catalogue: lavender polyester pantsuit, gold hoops swinging from her ears, lipstick bright as a tulip, clipboard in one hand and calm in the other.

"Hello, Mary," she says, her voice wrapped in kindness and certainty. "I'm Dianne. Let's get your car loan application started."

Just like that, in the stuffy air of a bank lobby, a shift in our family line. A seed is planted in the darkest night.

Maybe things can be OK. Maybe miracles wear lipstick and high heels and call you softly by your name. This woman, a kind stranger, becomes part of the foundation we'll build from. A golden thread pulled through the wreckage. A miracle blooming smack dab in the mud. Not a rescue. Not our salvation. Just a crack of light, bright enough to keep us moving forward.

Ruth on the Echoes in the Hallway

I roam freely through the corridors of Jen's mind,
her body, this home we share together.

Every hallway hums with stories,
some tender,
some terrible,
some downright miraculous and highly paradoxical.

Others stay sealed shut.
Pulsing low with steady sadness, that's where grief lives.
In there the air is thick with things we don't talk about.

There are rooms flooded with warmth, rebellion and
the relief of not having to perform.
I like to curl up and nap in rooms where sunlight spills
across the floor.
The rooms where our imagination runs wild and
leashless.
The ones where no one's trying to be good.
Or bad.
We just play.

We have freedom to roam.

In other rooms, shadows collect like webs.
A room of selves still too afraid to be seen.
The ones still hiding in the dark.
There are parts that bark.
Some that howl.
And some that bite.

I never force the door open.
I wait.
Patient at every threshold.
Present.
Until they're ready.
Until they need me to be ready for them.
Jen carries them all,
every tender, aching, hungry, silly, golden part,
a whole house alive inside one broken body.

Some rooms she visits often.
The familiarity comforts her.
Other doors she dead bolted long ago.
Keys buried in deep pockets she doesn't check.

Every room in this house belongs.
Every story counts.
Nothing is wasted here.
Our walls contract and contract with seasons.
Rooms change shape, appear and disappear
when she isn't looking.
That's the nature of a living house:
It mourns.

It dreams.
It breathes.
It lives.
And I,
I am a key, and the keeper of keys.
The soft watch stationed at every door hinge.
The guardian who knows each creak and every
shudder.

Together, we tend this house.
Our circle of selves.
Room by room.
Step by step.

Not to control.
Not to fix.
But to love.

And to listen.
And to remember:
Even the rooms filled with silence
have songs inside them,
waiting to be heard.

—*Ruth*

Chapter 2:

Dissolving

Jen — Winter 2022

We've always loved the New Year. In our family, it's a sacred little reset button. Iris says she'd rather celebrate it than her birthday. "It feels like starting fresh," she says every year. A chance to turn the page.

But this year? It feels like we're still stuck in the last chapter. I'm not teeming with the usual hope or optimistic resolutions. After everything, my own illness and pain, a pandemic still shaping our days, Iris's mom declining, and now Mama, sick in a house that's literally falling apart around her and her dogs, I wake up not with possibility in my heart, but with weight.

Last night was the first time in seventeen years Iris and

I didn't kiss at midnight. Normally, we fall asleep early with the TV turned up to muffle fireworks for the sake of our rescue dogs. Even in sleep, our lips manage to find each other, somewhere around midnight, a little lovestruck homing beacon. Not this time. I couldn't bring myself to wake her.

But this morning, she turned to me with sleepy eyes and smiled, "Where's my first kiss of 2022?"

I leaned into her like a wave returning to the shore. I need her like roots need dirt. Her kiss returns me back to my body, even if just for that split second. Her love fuels me.

I hadn't really slept. Not the kind that restores. I'd taken melatonin gummies, even popped a Benadryl at 3 AM., but every time I closed my eyes, I saw Mama in that hospital bed, vomiting, feverish, waning from us, from me, from Earth.

That's when Ruth took over our mind. She lit up our inner control room like NORAD tracking Santa's Christmas Eve deliveries: blinking maps of Mama's house, multi-layered to-do lists, real-time dog care logistics, pages of emotional triage strategies. Ruth doesn't pace nervously. She circles like a wolf checking the perimeter. She doesn't bark without reason. She listens to the rustling, internal and external, and makes a map of everything we need to do.

Mental gymnastics aren't anything new, I've been doing hard core training in disaster response since I was a baby. Most days the disaster is my own body, still navigating the fallout from that tumor that almost took me out. All the surgeries, all the radiation, left scars not just on my skin and inside my body, but on my hardwiring. On my soul. On the structure of who I am.

When we need clarity, Ruth is our researcher. The archivist. The strategist. She never lets a single thread drop. When I stop resisting her, when I lean into her wisdom, she becomes something else entirely: not a dysfunction, but a devotion. Not a disorder, but an ancestral instinct. Sometimes, a force of unbelievable will.

Hypervigilance gets a pretty bad rap. Most people treat it like a flaw, a pathology, something to hide or be ashamed of. But when you've survived what we've survived, you know it becomes something else. Lean into it enough, it becomes wisdom. A sacred alert system. A kind of devotion born from necessity, from protection, from not having the privilege to look away. A kind of love that puts itself between you and the door.

Ruth reminds me of that. We're in a conscious relationship now. I don't ignore her anymore. I admire her gifts, her shadow, her absolute refusal to rest when our perimeter feels breached.

She's not some forgotten dog stuck in the basement. She's my partner. My companion.

Part of my inner knowing. Part of my intelligence.

Happy to be here. The honor is mine.

Ruth teaches me how to hold our vigilance with reverence. Not too tight, not too loose. To hone the instinct without letting it run our whole show. We trust each other now. We trust our record of surviving. So many near-misses. All the bad nights we made it through. All the mornings we didn't think would come.

Still, this morning, our edge is sharper. There's a clarity running through me hot like wildfire. I don't know if it's Mama's condition or something cosmic, but I've never felt Ruth quite this vividly.

And I trust her. I need her.

I got you.

Most of my life, I didn't know her name. I just knew something was in me, curled near the door. Always watching. Always ready. Capable of incredible things.

Usually when we hit the Alabama state line, every part of my nervous system signals danger, danger! Turn around. But not today. Not now. I don't have the energy for running. I need a clean house inside myself if I'm gonna help clean the one Mama's been living in.

Frannie agrees to stay at the hotel with the dogs. She's content with snacks and a downloaded season of *Power Rangers*. There is a rare calmness wrapped around her. That alone feels like a miracle. I kiss the top of her head hard and say, "Thank you."

Iris and I have a plan. Mama can't come home to that house in the condition it's in. And even if my body is stitched together with pins and rods and good karma, we're gonna do whatever it takes to make things right, we just need help.

Mama's job as a dog sitter has brought her purpose since Lamar passed. A way to tether herself to the world on her own terms. She loved him with her whole being, and when he died, something in her detached. Not just grief, a dimming. A long exhale that never quite turned back into her vital breath. The light in her died with him. The version of her who belly-laughed at jokes just...thinned out like her head of silver hair that used to be so thick and wild.

She didn't disappear, but she did everything in her power to not be touched. Some people might label Mama a recluse, but for her, being left alone is the only way to exist. Not alone as in empty or unloved, just untouched. In her way, she's never truly alone. She lives with plants and animals wrapped around her like kin. But people? She keeps them outside. No visitors at the door. No one crosses the threshold of her house.

Pet sitting for these families brought new light into her life after Lamar died. They trusted her. They left her keys. Left her their hearts. Let her into their homes without judgment. Especially the Roberts family. They didn't just hire her, they relied on her. With their pets. Their schedules. Their routines. Their trust. They love her and she loves them.

This morning, we do another round of safety checks at Mama's, make sure the dogs have everything they need, and take them outside one by one on a leash. Then head to the Roberts' house to talk about the situation at Mama's house. Iris drives. Nina, the matriarch of the Roberts family, texts us not to ring the bell because Molly, their new rescue dog, doesn't like it. Then another text from her: **I love your mom so much.**

She really loves Mama. She's invited us to stay there, a generous offer, but there's no way. Not with our little crew of pee-pad aficionados and Frannie's unpredictable rhythms. And Mama? She would straight up raise right out of that hospital bed and murder me if one of our dogs pissed on The Robert's fancy rugs.

We're good at the hotel!

We pull into a swanky neighborhood, Hampton Cove. Waterfalls. Gates. Perfect topiary trees. The kind of community where patio furniture costs as much as cars. The Roberts' family home is stately, but warm. Familiar. Mama's been driving these roads for years on her own sort of patrols. As we walk in, the house glows with warmth and smells like vanilla. Yellow walls, the same color Mama used in her own living room. She rolled the paint on by herself last year at seventy-five years old, high up on a ladder like a woman with nothing to lose.

Nina and Terry greet us like we're old friends, hugs all around. Molly the dog offers a full-body wiggle. I'm pretty sure dogs sense that I have a dog living inside me, the air is full with care.

When Nina asks how Mama's doing, I don't sugarcoat it. "She's not well. She can't keep food down. Can't even drink water. They're keeping her at the hospital"

Their faces change. Worry settles over all of us thick like dust. My mouth is so dry I can barely get the right words out. I let all the worms out of the can, a bold move that seems like the right thing to do since they love Mama so much. We talk about boundaries. About the years I wasn't allowed in Mama's house. That I asked but I was turned away. I respected her boundaries, but I'm still not sure if that was compassion or a way of keeping my head in the sand.

Mama's rules are unquestionable. She doesn't explain them. She doesn't bend them. It's always been that way. And after a while, after enough no's stacked like bricks, I stopped asking to come inside her house. Not because I stopped wanting to. But because the asking itself became its own kind of wounding between us.

Ruth reminds me: *Tell them about the campaign.*

"I'm starting a GoFundMe," I say. "She can't come home to that house. She needs heat. Safety. Real help. There's been flooding every time it rains hard ever since they started building that development behind her house."

When I tell them there's been no central heat probably since Lamar died, Nina gasps. "She's just been using space heaters in every room?"

"Yep. The real problem? Burn marks on every outlet. Mama's house is a fire trap."

Nina and Terry spring into action. Handyman. Landscaper. HVAC referrals. Legal help for the flooding overflow. They open every door, offer every resource. I crack a joke in Mama's voice, I do a perfect imitation: "Jenny, don't go tellin' people about my business..." and Terry howls with laughter. Mama's body is in the hospital but her spirit is in the room with us, rolling her eyes no doubt, but grateful.

When we get up to leave, Ruth hums like a tuning fork through the metal rods of my spine.

We have work to do.

Nina walks us through the house, shows us the bathroom, laundry room, shower, just in case we ever need refuge. They both go on and on about their love for Mama and how important she is in their lives. Driving back, I feel some ease within me. We're not alone on this journey to help Mama. Then my phone rings.

"Nina?"

"Your mom can't come home to a cold house," she says. "Terry and I want to buy her a new HVAC system. We'll give you our card. Go to Lowe's. Today."

I put her on speaker. "Are you sure?"

"I insist."

Tears spilling. "That's thousands of dollars..."

"I know. And she needs it."

I can't speak. Iris reaches for my hand. We both cry. Something painfully tight lets go inside me.

I don't know how to receive generosity like this. Without offering something back. I'll return their generosity somehow.

People oughta know there are real good folks in the world who care. Who go above and beyond not for any other reason than they care. That's worth shouting from the rooftops!

I accept their gift. For Mama. For all of us. I hang up as we pass the waterfalls again on the way out of Hampton Cove. My hand is still on the phone. My throat is tight with something unspeakable. Not grief. Not a shock. Something else—the tenderness of being met. Of being seen, even when Mama's worst fear was being seen.

I press my palm to my chest, half expecting to find something new pulsing there. It's not just the HVAC. It's the way they didn't flinch. The way they just said yes. And for the first time, I think, maybe this year, this wild and weary new year, something good might have been sparked. We're not just trying to keep Mama alive. We're gonna help her live.

Ruth — 1980

very renovation starts with a demo. Not just of drywall or ductwork—but of beliefs. Old blueprints. Secrets passed down through bloodlines like heirlooms.

Jen's learning this now. That to rebuild a life, a house, a sense of self, you have to let the hurt crack you open first.

Let me take you back. Before our house could become a home, it became dangerous. Before we knew comfort, we memorized escape routes that freed us from screaming. Before we built anything new, we learned how to disappear, how to lie, and how to survive.

It's my job to protect. Especially on those hospital days. Cold exams. Endless questions. The needles. The way those doctors' hands, fingers, and brains claim her body like it belongs to them. It doesn't.

Does her body belong to her? To cancer? Or to those freshly washed hands tracing up and down along her snake-like spine, curved from so much radiation damage? They press, prod, and poke, unwelcome. She's not really sure who her body belongs to. Not when every appointment obscures the borders of what is hers and what is not. They treat her like land being surveyed. Objectified. Marked with a tattoo on her baby belly where the radiation field was. She loves the attention, though, uninvited as it is. When you don't have any sense of who you are, any identity will do. Even one built on being miraculous for being sick.

I watched those gloved hands reach in like they owned her. Watched the wires and metal snippers, watched worry unfold behind surgical masks at the sight of that giant tumor. They called it Stage III Neuroblastoma, cancer of the nerve tissue that filled her abdomen like it was trying to become a permanent part of her. It has already traveled to her lymph nodes. I was there when they cut Baby Jenny's belly open. I was there when they pinned her down with those straps to deliver radical doses of radiation. She screamed. We howled. No one ever saw me. But I was there, already circling. Already protecting.

Most hospital days Jen, now 7, and Big Brother, now 10, ride the city bus to get to appointments, paper bus passes in hand. Punch marked proof they belong somewhere. Proof someone was responsible for them. Big Brother is still a child himself, forced to take on too much. Little boy's feet forced into big man's shoes.

He doesn't complain about those shoes. He doesn't say they hurt to walk in. But the burden of those shoes shows in the way his body tightens when Jen falls behind all the time. He throws her the infamous Peer Stare, eyes so sharply focused they penetrate right through anything they peered at. Dad taught us how to use that like a tool—sometimes a weapon—against each other and the world. The weight of what Big Brother carries shows in how he memorizes bus routes and appointment times like their lives depend on it. Because they do, Jen's life depends on those checkups and Mama would kill him if anything happened. It shows in the way Big Brother stands too close to her at crosswalks, shoulders squared, still so small himself, just in case. He's a highly sensitive soul tasked with the impossible: Protecting his little sister from a world that keeps forgetting they're both kids. Sometimes he goes quiet for whole bus rides, eyes fixed on something far away outside the window.

California is home, the Bay Area to be exact. Some weekends Mama drove the kids to visit Grandma and Grandpa, and Mama's brothers and sisters who lived in houses tucked into the Santa Cruz mountains. We'd be driving up those winding roads, almost there, when just like clockwork, Mama's whole body changed. Her jaw grew tighter than its usual tight. Her voice dropped and she transformed into a different kind of animal, growling and firm, ready with a threat wrapped in an old worn out pillowcase.

She'd pull the car over, turn around real slow, eyes locked on Big Brother and Jen, "Not a word about your father, got it?" The air grew completely still. We knew exactly what she meant. Nothing about Dad's trips to jail. Nothing about staying home alone all the time. Nothing about the bruises that weren't on our skin, but that covered our hearts. *Only good things. Only smiles. Only the appearance of normal.*

It wasn't a suggestion. It was an order. It was family law etched into our bones. Break it, and we didn't just face consequences, we betrayed the whole delicate system keeping us from shattering.

So we became actors in Mama's play, a production about all the ways reality can be denied. Reporting stories that weren't real. Smiling like everything was fine, even as our guts twisted with the weight and worry of how difficult our lives were at home. We learned young how to split ourselves in half: the face we wore for the world and the truth that hid beneath it.

Behind all of it, Mama's love came on a tight leash. If we slipped up, cracked open even a sliver of truth, her rage would sweep over our whole house like fire out of control. Not just because we disobeyed, because we threatened the illusions created to survive.

Leveraging illusions is how we learned to survive. Not just while visiting Grandma's house, but everywhere we went as a family. We lived on smoke and mirrors and peanut butter sandwiches.

That summer peeled the lid off a new decade, with new ways to find fun. The neighborhood kids figured out how to turn trash into flight. They'd drag old waterbed mattresses from piles, fill them partway with air, then run full speed to crash on one end while some other kid braced on the other. The force would launch them into the air like human catapults! They'd land on the ground sometimes laughing, screaming, sometimes the wind knocked right out of their lungs. It was dangerous. It was wild. It was everything. That's how it was, kids inventing joy out of scraps, bruises blooming like medals, laughter louder than whatever was going on at home.

One day, when no old mattresses could be found, Mama happened to be in one of her paradoxical moods, the kind where love came wrapped in adrenaline. She drove Jen and Big Brother to the rear of a waterbed factory that sat behind a rusted fence in the industrial part of town. No questions, only forward motion. Mama and Big Brother exacted an unspoken plan, at least to Jen anyway. Mama parked next to the chain link fence. Big Brother climbed up, onto the car, and hopped over. Jen stayed hidden low in the backseat, eyes fixed on the blur and thrill of it all. She knew better than to ask questions.

Big Brother disappeared, then not long after reappeared with the stolen item in his hands, a plastic bladder, deflated and brand new! He threw it over the fence onto the ground, and then hauled it into the car. It didn't cost a dime. Just nerve, timing, and one of Mama's wild hairs. That first summer of the 1980's, neighborhood kids flew one by one like wild Muppets through the air.

Mama's doing everything. Working full time at an aerospace company. Going to night school at the community college. Jen and Big Brother wait around while she's in class, they're not supposed to be there on campus. But they are, there's no extra money for babysitters. So caretakers appear in the form of vending machines sometimes filled with forgotten change. They arrive as squeaky linoleum floors that smell like Pine-Sol.

They trail the janitor around like ducklings. He's a kind old gentleman with an Irish accent. He lets them push his cart. Clean chalkboards. Doesn't ask questions. Doesn't tell them they need to leave. Just nods and smiles when they fall into step beside him. On breaks, college students play chess, Big Brother joins in and they teach him how to play.

They don't talk down to him. They speak to him like he's their equal. Like they see him as he sees himself. An adult. This is what survival looks like for kids who don't belong anywhere: hovering near the warmth of strangers. Staying close to opportunities for change. Becoming really good at pattern recognition. Playing without being invited.

It's 1981, Jen is eight. Mama's off work and driving today, which is safer than riding with Dad, but still a rough ride. Jen stretches her whole body across the back seat of the compact car that the bank lady helped Mama buy. Adrenaline is still pacing through us. Hospital days do that. She studies power lines outside the car window shifting and weaving like we're living inside a puzzle. California winter sun splinters through like a kaleidoscope. The world outside sparkles and snaps, just like we do on the inside, we remain on high alert.

Mama took Jen to her routine appointment at the hospital. Which means not having to wait for the city bus with Big Brother, and probably stopping at McDonald's, Jen's favorite. A Happy Meal feels like magic: fries, a prize, and the paper thin illusion of being normal. Happy families eat Happy Meals. Plus, Mama usually makes her get water when they eat out, but Happy Meals come with a drink.

Waiting in line at the drive through, Mama's tongue lands harshly, "Whaddya want?" Jen knows she means to ask what she wants to order for dinner, but underneath, the question feels more like an existential inquiry into Jen's long list of ongoing medical and emotional needs. Mama's jaw stays clenched like it's holding back a tsunami while they wait for the food. On their way home, Mama's foot hits the brakes, hard, over and over, flinging Jen in the back like a rag doll. No apologies. No seat belt. No conversation. Just a tight field of silence that says *don't make it worse.*

When they arrive home, Mama jumps out of the car, slams the door hard, and storms inside like a woman on a mission. Jen lingers behind, glad to finally be home after another long day at the hospital. She's hungry! Hospital days require fasting for blood work. The car smells like salt and pickles. Happiness is right here, in the form of a Happy Meal box on her lap. Red. Square. Glossy. A tiny promise. She peeks inside: Napkins. Fries. Cookie. A cheeseburger wrapped neatly in yellow paper.

And then—YES! Underneath the burger, tucked in like a secret reward: the McWrist wallet. This is not just a prize. It's proof. Of survival. Of being worthy of good things. The full set of collectibles is complete. Ronald McDonald and Grimace pencil erasers. McTop. And now, the wallet. This is Jen. Miracle Child. Collector of scars, family secrets, and Happy Meal prizes.

Her stomach rumbles. She sees the VW in the driveway and gets hooked by that old familiar spark: Dad's home! It's been weeks since he's been around. Maybe things will be okay tonight...probably not. But maybe.

She grabs the box and cup of soda, heads inside, excited to show him her prize. He's gonna love it. He always makes her feel taller. That he cares about her, even when he can hardly remember who she is when he's drunk. Even if it's not true. She wants it to be true. More than anything she wants Dad's love. Mama always says Jen is like Dad. Big Brother is like Mama. The problem is that when Mama says that, it's tongued with an implication that Jen is broken like Dad.

When she walks through the front door Mama's voice explodes like a bomb right at Dad: "If you're gonna act like a dog, go sleep in the garage with the fucking dogs!"

Shrapnel everywhere. Dad's splayed out on the kitchen

floor, slurring, eyes locked on something only he can see. Invisible monsters again. The ones that live in the corners of every room in this house and haunt the folds of our family. Haunted his parents too, and their parents. Those monsters haunt all of us.

He uses his feet to push across the floor towards the garage belly up. No words. Just the slow retreat of a creature too drunk to run. Too drunk to care.

The garage, once his sanctuary for fixing Volkswagens, is now the den of collapse. After vanishing for days, sometimes weeks of gambling, stealing, using, this is where he crashes. Self-destruction threaded through his soul like hardwiring.

They were divorced when Jen was two. There was love once, but it died before Jen was born. Mama had the divorce papers served while Dad was in jail. One time he pawned everything—our couch, TV, our toys. Gone. Mama waited. When he came back, she knocked him out with a bottle of his own liquor. Put him in the hospital for a week.

Tonight is no different. He gambled again. Mama found the jar empty. Her strawberry planter raided. Money gone.

Jen sets the cup down, then scans the kitchen for an escape route through the battlefield, clutching the Happy Meal like a protective vest. But the bottom flaps open. Food crashes to the floor, a sad offering to the ground. She freezes. Eyes glaring on Mama. Then softening on Dad. She turns and scurries down the hallway.

She could stay hidden. She probably should stay hidden, retreat to her room. But the need to be close to Dad, to see if he's okay, pulls harder than any fear.

Mama's bedroom door slams in anger. Silence rolls thick like fog across the house. She's so mean to Dad, Jen doesn't understand why Mama makes him sleep in the garage. I know why, he's not safe. But Jen doesn't understand, she couldn't hear me back then. But I was there.

She tiptoes back out. Feet biting into the carpet like regret with teeth.

She tries to float. She cannot. She's not a ghost, as much as she wishes she were sometimes.

There it is in the kitchen. The McWrist wallet. Still wrapped in plastic. Still hers. The whole Happy Meal on the ground. Jen walks right past it, leaving her treasure, the final piece of the collection, on the ground. She slowly cracks the garage door where warm air meets her face. Dad's on the floor, a smile floating somewhere behind his eyes. She smiles back, hoping it means something. She steps closer. Touches him. Nothing.

She cries, "Dad?" He stirs. His face twists like the brown paper bag cinched at the neck of his bottle. He sees her crying and starts sobbing too. Sobbing like a child, to a child: "Don't be like me...I'm sorry."

She doesn't understand what he means, not really. But something inside her receives it like a secret code. She curls underneath the heavyweight of his arm. He smells like fermented grapes of Thunderbird wine and Pall Mall cigarettes. This becomes their shared signature scent, something she'll never forget. It's all they have between them.

He passes out again. She stays. Hungry. I gnaw at her gut, but being with Dad is way more important for her. There in the garage, next to our family's own one-man wrecking ball, Jen feels a strange kind of warmth. Like loyalty is its own kind of home. It's its own kind of razor-sharp safe place.

A dog's kind of love. My kind of love. Fierce. Unquestioning.

This is how Jen learned the rules of devotion. Not from

the people who stayed clean, sober, and standing upright, but from the ones we tried to hold up when they fell. We didn't learn the rules of life from the ones that stayed, we learned them from the ones that ran away.

I'm right there beside her. Always, though she's not aware of me yet.

We are shaped in this house. By that hallway. By floors that remember. By the garage. In the gaps between long silences and uncontrollable yelling and endless disappointments. In the moments when we shouldn't have had to choose, but did. By things we didn't understand, but felt anyway.

And we chose loyalty. We chose love. Even when love didn't, or couldn't, love us back. But we're learning. We're learning that vigilance is an instinct. That loyalty, even when painful, is a kind of strength.

The echoes between Jen and me grow longer each year. Every room. Every hallway. Every crack in our floors. Every act of survival that should have bound us closer becomes something that rips us apart with forgetting. The kind of forgetting that comes when pain is carried for too long.

I don't blame her for pushing me away. How could I? She did what she had to do to survive.

But I remember. I remember the first time I yowled from the inside, her baby fists curled in rage, her screams unrelenting. I remember curling up behind her ribs, keeping watch over her when no one else did. I remember holding the perimeter when all she had left was breath.

Years later, with the help of the pediatric oncologist who saved our life, Dr. Sarah Donaldson, I pulled our medical records. I had to see it with my own eyes. Confirm what we already knew in our bones. What was done. What it took. Radiation doses meant for grown men, mapped across our body that couldn't even sit up yet.

I'll share more another time. Some things have to ripen underground before they're ready to rise. But know this: we survived numbers that should have ended us. And not just survived, we remembered. Every single beam of light that burned its way in. Every beam that gave us life with a lifetime of conditions.

She doesn't always feel me. But I'm here. Not lurking. Not haunting. Just waiting. Just protecting all sides, like a good dog does.

These are our beginnings. We were born in the wreckage. Dad passed out in the garage. In and out of jail. Uneaten Happy Meals. Mama's contorting of reality. Vending machines and strangers acting as babysitters. Kids forced to be adults. But love was born there too. In the staying power of something loyal, something vigilant—circling on the edge of so many disasters. I was watching. Protecting. Mapping our way to safety. Again and again.

Chapter 3:

Fracturing

Jen — Winter 2022

Iris is my better half. Better in the way a milkshake is already perfect, but then you add whipped cream, rainbow sprinkles, and a cherry on top. She's all of it—the soft sweetness, the spark, the final flourish that makes the whole thing sing. When she heads back to Atlanta Sunday night for work, early, to beat the incoming snow, I feel the shift the moment she pulls away. Even though we're texting nonstop, even though we are and will forever be connected, the distance feels as wide as the 173 miles between us.

Iris is not just my emotional anchor, she's also our family muscle. The picker-upper. The lift-it, move-it, climb-on-the-ladder-and-fix-it partner. Psoriatic arthritis chews my joints. My spine is fused from neck to pelvis—rods, pins, screws. That's what happens when a baby's spine gets radiated, it degenerates. Titanium scaffolding keeps me upright. I move through pain every single day, in a body that keeps going even under enormous pressure.

Breathing hurts sometimes. Simply raising my arms to reach for a hug provokes unbelievable muscle contractions. I've learned how to adjust and readjust myself in tiny, invisible increments, micro-movements, like tuning a broken body harp that no one else can hear. But I hear it. I hear them. My own internal jam band of musicians, busy playing instruments out of broken parts. Banging out impromptu songs of survival. I call them The Chronic Pains, I'll tell you more about them someday.

And Iris? She's been there for every part of it. She knows our songs, the instruments, the pains. She helps me put my socks on. Reaches for the top shelf. Carries the weight of all the things that steal the little energy I have. Never once with resentment. Though she does give me that simple look when I push too hard. Which, let's be real, is a lot!

Her absence presses against the edges of everything. Our hotel room. Frannie. My spine. My mind. My heart. This is the moment where I gotta dig deep. Be the strong one. Handle the chaos of Mama's dogs, Mama's house, Mama's sickness, plus Frannie, our two weenie dogs, and my own body, which barely holds itself up on a good day. I'm standing in need of a bonafide miracle. Probably a dozen of them.

Right now? I'm all lit up, buzzing from the inside out like a broken power line in an Alabama windstorm. Ruth is fully at the helm, my inner guide, pacing the hallways inside me. I feel her eyes scanning our perimeter, measuring the odds, inventorying every pantry and closet in this house we share. I can barely feel my body, that's how alive I am in this alertness. That's how high the stakes feel. That's how very good Ruth is at her job. Hypervigilance, it's a bubbly cocktail of stress chemicals and pristine pattern recognition. It's a hell of a drug!

Even with Iris gone, Frannie is rising up in her own ways. She's meeting the moment with a kind of maturity we haven't always seen in her. She's giving Wicky his meds without reminders. She's snacking, mostly responsibly. She offers up her savings, two weeks' allowance tucked into a crinkled Ziploc bag, for Grandma's house fund. Her generosity undoes me in the best way possible. It's amazing how our loop of love always comes full circle.

Mama's still in the hospital, very sick. She can't keep anything down, not even water. Ice chips and wet lemon-flavored sponge-on-a-stick are all she can manage to hold in her mouth. Her frame, already thin, is shrinking. She's dropped fifteen pounds since that hiatal hernia surgery. Her eyes have become sunken like moon crags, her voice threadbare.

The surgeon comes into the room and shrugs. "Everything looks fine. Her intestines just need to wake up."

Just?

Ruth files that under: *Bullshit we need to research.* Because let me tell you: when someone can't eat, can't walk, can't sit up for more than five minutes, and they're saying it's fine? It's not just fine. Nothing is fine. Plus if they discharge her, she'll be coming home to a house that isn't ready.

If she doesn't let us stay with her? Then what?

This might be the only sliver of time we have to change anything.

Over the weekend, Iris returned and we made some headway. She cut out the water-damaged wallboard in the sunroom, sprayed for mold, and patched the bottom with plywood. I disinfected every reachable surface, vacuumed years of dog fur, scoured the kitchen, unclogged bathroom drains. My body screamed, but I managed to stay in perpetual motion, driven by the commitment to make things better.

I launched the GoFundMe:

Mary's Healing & House Fund
The one who is always there for everyone and all animals is in need of our help!
My mama is Mary Sloan of Owens Cross Roads, Alabama. She is a proud Marine Corps veteran, seventy-six years young, and a longtime animal rescuer and adopter in the Huntsville area. There's not a square mile of town she hasn't shown up in to help a feral cat, give a stranger a ride, or scoop up a dog someone left behind. She has adopted out hundreds of animals in the Tennessee Valley area...

The response was immediate. Donations. Messages. Shares. Prayers. Bonafide miracles showing up one by one.

Iris returned to Atlanta. Frannie's settled at the hotel with the pups nestled around her, TV on low, everything within reach. It's not perfect, but it'll hold for now. Ruth and I? We get to work.

First priority: fencing. Mama can't walk six dogs on leashes. I can't either. A fenced yard will change everything. North Alabama Fence says they can come Thursday or Friday, weather depending.

Next: heat. Nina and Terry insisted on buying her a

new HVAC system. Not just a unit—but ducts, thermostats, installation. The works. Their generosity—instant, whole-hearted, no questions asked—the first miracle we never saw coming.

Then: the junk haulers. I hired a team to help clear out two rooms that haven't been touched in years. One room used to be my brother's. Later it became mine, that's where I lived when I returned at twenty, shattered, trying to take care of Frannie. Now? I see it as a room for me again. A refuge.

I imagine seafoam green walls, white trim, with cool light pouring through the broken windows. A temporary place where I can rest. Like an island postcard in the middle of rural Alabama. Maybe something like you'd see on Fantasy Island?

I open the door and nearly fall over. We're a long damn way from the beach.

The room is a warehouse of boxes, yellowed papers, and broken furniture. It smells like old dust and the kind of for-getting that turns into hoarding. I start small. One box. One trash bag. One stack at a time.

I work from a wheeled office chair with a broken seat back, rolling across the floor like steering through icebergs, there's more than meets the eye in every pile. Ruth keeps the rhythm. She hums. Directs. Warns me not to push too far.

Then I found it, the rat. At the back of the closet, nestled in shredded newspaper, a small gray body curled in a well-crafted nest. Dead. Engulfed by white wriggling maggots—alive. Life eating life.

Ruth and I pause.

We don't panic. We feel reverence. A creature lived here. A creature died here. It was trying to survive. Just like mama. Just like us.

I Google it. How to kill maggots in a dead rat. Bleach.

With bleach in hand, I hold my breath and pour, gagging as I burst into tears, not from the grossness of it, but from the burn of bleach mixing with instant tenderness. It's never my plan to hurt anything. Even larvae. Even the rat. I thank Mama's unseen roommates for their lives. I know what it's like to survive in a house that's falling apart.

I know this too: life doesn't end. It transforms. That's alchemy. The rat becomes maggots. The maggots become flies. The flies return to the cycle. So will I. Once dead, I might come back as a weenie dog, a Florida snail, or maybe a vigilant rat myself. Still caring. Still protecting what matters. That, too, is devotion. That, too, is love.

Ruth — 1983

Jen's always had a soft spot for the ones no one else sees. The ones mostly overlooked. She didn't look away because she always felt like she was overlooked too. Even the rat. Even the larvae. Even the parts of herself that came out sideways, howling and uncontainable. She doesn't flinch from the mess of life, she whispers to it. Cleans what can be cleaned. Blesses what can be blessed. But before all this, before the bleach, rat and larvae, there were trees. The trees held her from the get-go. Let me take you there. Back to where it began. Back to the girl on the swing, flinging songs into the forest with a heart wild enough to believe they might be heard.

It's the height that stirs her. Or maybe it's the way the redwoods sway together in the wind, dancing with rhythm older than language. Their silence isn't empty; it's full of breath, full of presence. Spinning beneath them on that wooden swing, Jen feels something she rarely does: tall. Grounded. Seen.

For a kid who always comes up short, the forest at her grandparents' house in Boulder Creek is a sanctuary. A cathedral without walls. Grandpa Big John hung a swing from one of the soaring branches. A simple board on thick chains. She climbs onto the swing, shifting her crooked body back and forth as it lifts her towards the canopy and spins us in wild, dizzying circles. Her legs pump and her lungs sing.

She belts out songs to the trees, spontaneous love notes flung skyward *I love you, I love you, I love you!* Her words get caught in the branches, tucked into ancient redwood bark like secrets. And sometimes, when the wind hits just right, she swears they sing back: *We love you too.*

They feel like a chosen family. Real. Rooted. Reverent.

There was a similar warmth on occasional weekend visits with Dad, who lived out at the edges of Agnews State Hospital, a sprawling campus turned half-ghost town, half community for folks the world was fine to throw away. She never went inside the units where he worked. Big Brother did. She only went to Dad's apartment, tucked in a back corner of a very strange institutional world, the breeze always smelled like bleach. The palm trees creaked because they held too many secrets. The maze of roads carried the sound of something still alive, but barely.

Dad started working there as a janitor. His presence calmed the patients. Most were developmentally disabled, some locked up in there for reasons society wouldn't name.

Hospital administrators noticed something in Dad. Potential. They invested in him. Paid for his training to become a licensed psych tech. He was trying, in his own clumsy, haphazard way, to become more than he'd been. Responsible. Sober. Employed. All things he struggled with. He never paid Mama child support. Not one dime.

In that tiny apartment on the campus of Agnews, Dad let Jen be fully herself. Let her use his computer, dot matrix printer, and a software program called Print Shop to create long colorful banners. He always let her talk too loud, laugh too hard, take up all the space Mama always shrank from. He praised her creativity. Like it was something good. Like her ideas mattered.

I remember the mousse fiasco. Jen didn't mean anything by it. Just a daughter playing beauty parlor in a one-room apartment that smelled like cherry vanilla pipe tobacco and days old coffee. She found a can of mousse on the bathroom counter, ironic since Dad was mostly bald,, and decided his beard was the perfect canvas for her latest creation. It was thick and wild and begged for reinvention. She giggled, scrunching and swirling, fingers full of foam, sculpting his face into something glorious, big and totally ridiculous. And he let her. He sat right there on the edge of his bed, legs and arms crossed, letting love take the shape of hair art.

She didn't know the mousse had alcohol in it. Didn't know Dad was on Antabuse. Didn't know that her small hands covered in alcohol could set off a chemical storm in his body.

But they did.

That night, he got so sick. Violently, gut-wringing sick. He made it to the bathroom just in time to puke, barely. Jen stood in the doorway, confused, asking if the food they ate made him sick. He shook his head between heaves and managed to rasp, "It's the mousse. It's okay. I forgot to check the label."

She blinked. "You're puking because of your beard?"

He nodded and shot a weak little smile.

She sat on the floor outside the bathroom while he threw up everything he had in his stomach. He didn't tell her to go to bed. He didn't say she'd done anything wrong.

In the morning, the sun painted the edge of the one windowsill golden with California light. Dad hugged her tight. Called her his Miracle Child. His Jen-A-Bug. She nuzzled into him like it was safe to belong. And for that moment, it was.

"It was good while it lasted, your beard creation," he laughed, wiping at his face, still red. He wasn't mad. Not even close. He knew what it meant to try and do the right thing and mess up.

And I saw it. I always saw it. The way she tried to create beauty in broken places. The way he tried to hold steady, even while puking his guts out from that Antabuse. Two humans loving each other in their own strange ways, from inside their own chaos.

It wasn't a greeting card father-daughter relationship. But it was their truth. And truth is something I track better than most.

Dad was a long way from perfect. He was held together by pain and addiction, compulsion and endless regrets. But he never made Jen feel like she was too much. Not that night. Not that morning. Not even when she made him sick by accident. That meant something. It still does.

She carried that memory forward through time, one small room tucked away in her house. Proof that love can survive in a mess. That people didn't have to be perfect to be cared for.

I remind her of that, she forgets sometimes. I open that room in dreams, his laugh, that golden ray of sunlight, the feeling of being a Miracle Child. That kind of love—real, busted, human love, it never leaves. It becomes part of our house. Part of what holds us together.

In 1983, Mama received a job offer she couldn't refuse: a major promotion halfway across the country in Austin, Texas. A clean break. A new beginning far from the wreckage of her marriage to Dad and our house walls soaked in booze and bad decisions. She takes the job. Dad doesn't stop her, and stays back in California.

Texas means different things for the three of them. For Mama, it's a real milestone. Her own house. Her own paycheck. Her own rules. She even buys full-size arcade games and has them delivered upstairs to their new game room, Asteroids and Galaga. For the kids, part reward, part babysitters. Living with Mama was a lot like trying to plant a garden during a drought. There was sun, there was soil, but the water came in flash floods, unpredictable and fierce.

For Big Brother, now thirteen, the move comes as a relief. It's a reprieve from always taking care of his little sister. At first he struggles, but then a school psychologist recognizes his hidden intellect. He transfers from a school for high-risk kids to a new school, with teachers who recognize his gifts. His life starts to open and he begins to thrive.

For Jen, it's a rupture. She's ten. Torn from her forest family. From trees that knew her name, that said they loved her. From Dad who, despite his chaos, was hers. Their connection, sporadic, thin, but vital, was now gone.

She calls his number again and again. The rotary phone

wears a groove from her finger. The sixteen-foot coiled cord tangles around her legs and feet like a snake. No one answers. Just ringing. Then a beep. Then silence. Then nothing. She doesn't know yet that the only way out of a Chinese finger trap is to press inward.

They become Texas latchkey kids. Mama works long hours. They live on microwave pancakes and frozen dinners. Shop for food at Warehouse Grocery late at night when the store is nearly empty of other shoppers. Mama avoided talking to strangers unless it was absolutely necessary.

We'd float through the aisles like a family of midnight ghosts, Mama practically invisible. Lights too bright, cold humming all around. Jen didn't want to disappear. She liked people, and people liked her, she was hungry for attention, Mama barked orders like we were in bootcamp, "Go ask how much this is." A few minutes later, "Find someone and ask where the day old bread is!"

Mama's demand for invisibility pushes the kids forward over and over into grown-up tasks. They always do the talking. Big Brother flanks the cart, watching the math. Mama keeps her distance from everyone, silent, thick like fog until it's time to check out. She rips out the check to pay and hands it over, no smile. No small talk. Transactional. Matter of fact.

Christmas was hard. Not because of what happened, because of what didn't.

The house grew quiet. Gifts came, rarely wrapped. The tree leaning over, half dead from neglect, lights blinking like they knew something about the celebration wasn't real. Wasn't home. Mama tried to get into the holidays, sometimes. Jen felt the shift in her chest before December even arrived, a darkness that crept inside Mama and froze her right up. A cold snap that made it hard to breathe. The house shut down in winter.

Easter? It was like a sudden breath of fresh air. Baskets filled with bright green plastic grass appeared. Then disappeared when Mama hid them in the backyard. Fancy chocolate eggs. A wash of springtime colors and sunshine. Suddenly everyone could breathe easier without knowing why.

The contrast left a mark, one that returned year after year. The weight of winter. The lift in spring. The family wouldn't name that pattern for decades. But it lived under their skins, in their cells, in the way the house curled up tight in December and opened like crocus in April.

Typical mornings in Austin smell like scorched syrup and burnt cardboard. Jen learns to drown frozen microwaved pancakes in super hot syrup. They soften right up. A survival trick. A culinary art.

Her newest caretaker is the television, their living room always hums with noise. No one's watching her, so the TV does. She falls into the weird, wonderful world of unsupervised 80s programming, a flickering portal she climbs right through, barefoot, invisible, but somehow also seen.

Her favorite escape hatch: *Fantasy Island.* A seaplane arrives like clockwork, its twin engines slicing through the blue sky. The cliffs rise, impossibly lush, cradling the island like a secret. Mr. Roarke throws open the shutters, white suit gleaming. Tattoo rings the bell from the tower: *"The plane! The plane!"* and just like that, she's gone. No longer a kid alone in Texas. No longer waiting for someone to notice. Now she's somewhere people care. Somewhere she's expected. Longed for even. Every guest on the island matters. Every arrival is met with fanfare. For the length of an episode, she's not alone. She's part of something. A world where dreams unfold and wrongs get righted. A place where her deepest desire isn't too much. That's the whole point. Fantasy Island is more than a show, it's an invitation. An imaginary place of belonging, not just watched, but absorbed, cell by cell, dream by dream.

In the large walk-in closet in her bedroom upstairs she finds even more belonging in a hammock fashioned from a flat bed sheet. She ties knots on all four sides, and climbs on in, knees curled up to her chest. Hammock swaying gently, like someone's rocking her, but no one shows up. Darkness wraps around, close, still, keeping her company.

For Jen, that hammock becomes a hospital bed. A place where absence gets noticed. Where tenderness is the protocol. Nurses appear like clockwork: soft-voices, clipboards, concern. All smiles, checking vitals with imaginary thermometers and whispering affirmations as they fluff pillows. Visitors bring handmade cards and cafeteria trays. She scripts it all out loud, line by line:

"We miss you at school."
"We brought chocolate milk."
"You're so brave."

She mouths the words right back to herself, rehearsing what it might feel like to be held and seen in that kind of light. Being sick meant being special. Being sick meant someone showed up. So she shows up for herself. Even in make-believe. Especially in make-believe, she builds a whole world where care becomes predictable. Alone in that bedroom closet there's a private stage, an imaginary place where she is the patient and the healer. The one who wants love and the one who gives love.

There was one day Jen stayed home from school. Said she felt sick, but mostly she was just sad. Alone in the quiet house, heart too full and too empty at once. She got dressed up in her fancy nightgown, the pink one with the satiny ribbon and the tiny rosettes at the collar. A costume for being seen. Then she stood at the top of the stairs, took a breath, and flung herself down like a body in a made-for-TV movie.

Then she called Mama at work. Said she'd fallen. Said she needed an ambulance. Said it just like she practiced in her head. Mama? She believed her. She called the ambulance. But never came home to check on Jen.

But the paramedics came. Lights spinning, boots clomping, big hands lifting her little wrists. She got the whole parade. Vitals, questions, that familiar smell of rubber gloves. And yeah, it was funny, but it was actually a flare in the sky from a girl trying to say: Hello, I'm here...someone please pay attention to me.

There are mother-daughter fights born of teenage angst that are ordinary and to be expected. Theirs were not that. These were scorched-earth battles. Guttural. Teeth-bared on both sides. Mouths foaming. Room-shaking, doors slamming furious anger. Mama calling Jen a liar, like her no-good Dad. A loser. A freak. Too emotional. Out of control. Always too loud. Mama grabs her ears like she's in pain when Jen laughs too loud. Her tone runs thick with disappointment, sharp with judgement.

Soft-faced and wild-hearted, Jen screamed back with every ounce of breath she had: "I hate you! I fucking hate you, Mama!"

Then night would come. Like a toy soldier, her feet carried her right back to Mama's room. Jen hated to sleep alone, so she curled in bed next to Mama, right after the two of them just set each other on fire. There was no winning in this house. No peace. Only the push and pull of survival wrapped in endless paradox.

Mama had a way of slipping tiny knives into her tender mind. Not intentionally, it was happening without awareness. Those knives were forged somewhere. Jen's grandma was tuned to a mad frequency no one else heard. She saw things that weren't there. Her nickname was Wild Rose, and for good reason. She was creative. Obsessive. Often cruel. She shrieked all hours of the night in screaming fits that kept the whole house awake. Grandma yelled right through their childhood, filling their house with fury so unrelenting and sharp it carved permanent grooves into every sibling's skin.

Mama grew up in a house of painful noise. Jen came out of her womb crackling with life, loud in joy, loud in pain. Mama tracked that loudness like the return of a storm she'd barely survived. She didn't know how to hold it. She was afraid of it. She tried to silence it. Not because there was anything wrong with Jen's light, but because it reminded her of something awful and all-consuming she couldn't escape as a child. At least until she was old enough to leave home for the Marine Corps.

Jen's glittering, shape-shifting creativity was treated like one big joke. An irritation. Every bright idea was twisted into selfishness. Every drawing or story or silly made up song turned into something to question.

"You think you're special? That's your problem right there. Always needing attention."

That was the pattern. Mama honed in on where the shine was bright in Jen, and stomped it out before it got too cozy.

That said, here's what I've come to understand: Mama was trying really hard to hold together a house that caught fire a long time ago. She'd been burning up in the heat of her own stories. Her own pain. On some level, she was spooked by the light of the children she brought into the world. She thought if she kept the house dim enough, it might not show the cracks in her own foundation.

Still, it hurt. Jen stopped showing Mama things she made. I grew bigger, louder. Someone had to bark back. Someone had to remember what our light looked like.

Shame moved into our house early. Pain settled over all of us like dust in the corners. Self-doubt became the air we breathed. We learned intelligence could be twisted, made to look like arrogance. That love might follow harshness, but harshness always came first.

I kept watching through it all, nose pressed to the edge of our life, wanting to change our course, to break the spell that she wasn't good enough. But I was just Ruth. Just a dog on the inside endlessly barking in our house that was on fire too.

Mama kept striking matches in the dark, trying to make a way through life.

It was Austin, Texas, in the middle of the 80s, dry heat and payphone booths, roller skating rinks with endless circles jamming to Madonna and Prince. Wide belts, brightly colored converse high tops, big hair and even bigger feelings, and Jen, at thirteen, was right in the thick of it.

She tried to give herself a mohawk one day, wielding a pair of dull scissors and not nearly enough mirror. It was a disaster, especially in the back. Mama opened the bathroom door to see what she was up to, took one hard look, and rolled her eyes so far back they nearly got stuck.

She didn't yell, just snapped, "Jesus Christ!" grabbed the scissors, and cleaned up the mess, quiet, practical, precise.

She didn't say you look cool or I understand why or I love you. But she did fix the back. And in our house, that meant a lot.

Jen and Mina became fast friends in that all-in, all-consuming way only teenage girls can be. Matching thrift store skirts one day, cut-off T-shirts the next, safety pins, and jelly shoes finished off with the brightest eyeshadow they could find. They were mixtapes of rebellion and endless cans of Aqua Net hairspray.

They were pretending to be cool. Heck, they were cool, in that awkward, electric, scrappy 80s kind of way, piecing themselves together from secondhand stores and raw instincts.

In 1986, when the movie *Pretty in Pink* came out, they saw themselves in it. But where Andie had a dad who was soft, Jen lived in a house full of hard edges and a lot of silence. She stayed at Mina's house whenever she could. Mama was fine with it, Jen was out of her hair at least.

Mina's mom cooked big meals, offered Kool-Aid, and didn't ask questions. She gave Jen a towel without being asked for one. Her parents always smiled when the twosome came barreling through the door. Jen didn't realize what that warmth represented, but I did. I felt the ache settle into our ribs like a sad second heartbeat. Mama took care of our needs, but she didn't have space for warmth. By fourteen, *The Lost Boys* hit theaters and something shifted. Jen and Mina were sure they were vampires. And not in a costume-store kind of way. They didn't *play* at it—they *were* it. Real life vampires, in their minds. They roamed downtown Austin like nocturnal queens, underdressed and overstimulated, talking big, laughing loud, staying out too late. Nobody was watching. Nobody told them no.

There was danger, yes, lots of it, but there was also joy. Sticky, sweaty, electric teenage joy.

They'd trade Walkman headphones back and forth, always *The Cure, Depeche Mode*, sometimes *New Order*. The music wasn't just a soundtrack. It was a magic spell. It made everything feel bigger, sadder, more important than it was.

They stole time. They tried on personalities like clothes. They kissed each other and kissed boys they weren't sure they liked just to see what it felt like.

All the while, I was there. Not judging. Just staying close. Because sometimes the most sacred thing you can do is let a girl stay wild when the rest of her world is trying to tame her. They weren't bad. They were *alive*. I loved them for it. Jen barely attends middle school. Mina goes to a different school, which opens the door to a new friend, Brenda. She dares Jen to go further. They love the thrill of getting away with things. Anything. Backpacks become heist bags. The grocery store is their target. Candy bars, Garbage Pail Kids, Trapper Keepers, anything shiny, sweet, or forbidden. They learn how to slide things into their pockets without looking down. Without looking around. How to act casual when their hearts are pounding out of their chests.

Then Mama's gold ring disappears. Jen sells it to some older guys downtown to buy weed. It was a dare, and she never backs down. Every time, the stakes get higher, the voice inside louder. Not my voice, that impulsive and undeniable hum in her bloodline—go further, don't feel, don't flinch. Her world has too many edges that she doesn't know how to soften, so she gets edgier.

Jen starts dropping tiny paper doses of LSD while riding around for hours on city buses. The world around melts and morphs, lights bending while she and Brenda laugh until

their ribs hurt, Sometimes they scream, or cry about nothing at all. Everything is numb and strange. They sit and talk
for hours on bus benches, hot metal and peeling paint under
their thighs. No one really notices them downtown, and they
love it. It's freedom.

I stay curled up right beside her at those bus benches,
invisible, but vigilant. My head on her arm. Eyes on the
street. She didn't talk to me then. Didn't know I was there, I
never blamed her for not reaching out for me.

She skips school for days, sometimes weeks at a time.
She misses more school than she attends. Tells Mama she's
sick. Mama doesn't put up much of a fight. Just tells her to
stop calling her so much at work.

No one's asking where the pain goes. But I knew. I always
knew. She wasn't bad. She was just surviving one skipped
day of school at a time. I followed, tail low, making sure she
didn't go numb completely.

She fades into swirls of New Wave music, hair dye, weed,
smudged eyeliner, everything black, intense, broken and
pretending too hard to be too cool. Her body becomes a
background object. Her mind becomes a carnival of flash-
ing lights, a hall-of-mirrors, one big joke. Mama's words
keep looping over and over, too loud, too fast. No exit signs
marked. I was barking, but only on the inside, where no one
could hear me.

She starts cutting herself in secret, alone locked in the
bathroom. Blades stripped from disposable razors get pried
loose with trembling fingers. The bathroom becomes a
ritual site: the door is locked, lights dimmed, the whir of the
exhaust fan steady in the background. No one's knocking.
No one's coming. And for once, that's a relief. The world,
always so loud, so chaotic, narrows to a single point: skin,

breath, sting. Her focus sharpens. Her breathing slows.

Blood becomes a broken language, clearer than words, cleaner than pain. It says what she can't. It bleeds out what got stuck inside. Not just sadness. Not just anger. Not just loneliness. All of it. The ache of wanting to matter. The confusion of growing up without a map. Some rooms she had to survive without me, but I never left her side.

Cutting was a release. A return to gravity. Something she controls because everything else is out of control. It's not about wanting to disappear. It's about wanting to appear. To feel...alive. Real. Like maybe there's still some body underneath all the noise in her head.

She tells wild stories to friends. Dresses loud. Can be a bully. Becomes a magnet for bullies.

When she hears a group of girls plans to beat her up after school, she panics. Tells the principal she might die. "You know I had cancer, right?"

He interviews the girls one by one. A big mistake. Word spreads, Jen's dead meat after school and everybody's going to be there.

So she swallows two fistfuls of Tylenol in the bathroom. Maybe she wants to die. Maybe she just wants to escape the beating. She ends up in the ER with a stomach pump.

Mama's only question: "Whaddya you do to deserve that ass beating?"

Jen never returns to that middle school. What follows is a carousel of residential placements—each one promising something, then taking something else.

First: Shoal Creek Hospital. A 30-day inpatient program for kids with good insurance. Carpeted hallways. Soft lighting. Group therapy in beige rooms with folding chairs and dry-erase boards that smell like lemon cleaner. The food is good—real mashed potatoes, not the instant kind. There's even a pool. She makes friends fast. Plays the part. Takes antidepressant meds without complaint. Follows the rules. It's almost paradise.

Then: home. Back into the old house with the same fights. The same long silences. The same undercurrents of push and pull.

Then she's caught stealing jeans at the mall. The police take her to jail downtown and then they call Mama, who initially refuses to pick Jen up, "She made her own bed, she can lay in it."

Then: back to Shoal Creek. A new bed, this time different meds.

A new label: Mood Disorder. She wonders if anyone ever leaves this place without a label that sticks like a wad of chewed up gum on the sole of their life.

Then: Austin State Hospital. Insurance runs out. No more carpet. No more softness. Here, "acting out" gets you *popped*, slammed down by staff, strapped to a gurney, and injected with Thorazine until your world goes underwater. Jen learns the rules fast. How to keep her hands visible. How to walk in shoes with no shoe laces. That even bad attention is still attention. I watched her disappear behind her eyes. I stayed, I always do.

Then: Teen Connection. A temporary shelter. No one stays long enough to make friends. Girls come and go. She's forced to go to public school in Sherman, Texas. It doesn't take long before she's marked again for an ass beating, for her clothes, her posture, for always trying too hard to fit in. It never works. She refuses to go back to public school. Another failure. Another exit strategy. Another move.

Finally, a bed opens at Waco Center for Youth.

Mama's new boyfriend, Lamar Cecil Sloan, is a hand-some man that looks like he belongs in Hollywood movies. He drives a giant Georgie Boy RV. It looks like a dinosaur from the outside, bright stripes and an awning, and inside, it weirdly feels like a small home. Jen climbs aboard and feels something unfamiliar: space that doesn't reek of tension. It smells like sun-warmed plastic, maybe a hint of pine-scented air freshener or something clean like that. She exhales air in a way she didn't know she was holding.

On the way, they stop at the outlet mall. Lamar buys her boots. Not ones Mama picks, her choice, thick, black boots with snakelike laces and heavy soles that make her feel tall. Solid. Like someone who could walk into a room and really be seen.

Then they hit Dairy Queen. He lets her order whatever she wants. A Coke. A chocolate-dipped ice cream cone. Mama always made her get water. Said soda was too expensive. Said dessert was only for special occasions. But here, in this booth with red plastic seats and the hum of the soft-serve machine, Jen gets to just be a kid. A full one. For a moment.

At a rest stop about an hour away from the newest place-ment, Mama sits up front sorting through the AAA map book reviewing the route they'll take after they drop Jen off. Lamar moves to the kitchen area and pulls out a plastic bag full of fruit, strawberries, pineapple, bananas, and starts pre-paring and slicing each offering, one by one. "You like fruit salad?" "I think so." No fanfare. Just care. He hands her the fresh-cut salad on a Styrofoam plate, fruit arranged like it matters. Like she matters.

No one's ever made her fruit salad before. No one's ever made food for her like that: simple, thoughtful, offered with quiet tenderness. Mama usually ate in her room alone, door shut with the TV on. The kids fended for themselves in front of the living room TV. Meals were more like a scavenger hunt than getting actual nourishment.

But this, this feels like something sacred. Not the fruit really. The gesture. The way he peeled the bananas so gently. The way he smiled softly and then asked, "You want more?" and meant it. It's not the food that fills her, it's the way it's prepared and offered with care.

She decides right then that anyone who worries that much about fruit must be okay. Must be safe. And I agree with that.

Waco Center for Youth looks more like a college campus than a lock-up. Red brick buildings. Green sprawling lawns. Long sidewalks that fork off toward cottages named by number.

Cottage 14 is the one for the worst kids. The ones who fight, run away, or self-harm. The ones with nowhere to go. It's kind of like Fort Knox, but quieter. Inside the halls are lined with doors that lock from the outside. The air smells like cleaning solution and sweaty teenage bodies, overhead lights sigh like they're tired of being on all the time.

Outside the cottages, kids roam the campus in supervised clusters. They walk to therapy. To the cafeteria with its plastic trays and vending machine grape juice. To the gym, where the sound of volleyballs and basketballs echo like gunshots against the high ceiling. They have *some* freedom. Which means: an opportunity to run. To rebel. Test the rules to see if anyone will come after them.

They call it ULing—Unauthorized Leave. Slip past the boundary line, and staff are legally barred from chasing. Beyond that point, you belong to the police. It's a wild goose chase, but I marked every path so I could lead her back if we needed it.

Jen runs. Gets caught. Goes back to Cottage 14. Gets popped.

The pop isn't just restraint, it's punishment with a medical face. A chemical straightjacket. Injected sedation. Thorazine sleep. I was there. Just, further back. She ULs again. Sometimes the only way to cry for help is running in the opposite direction.

Jane, her therapist, always seemed kind. That was the trick of it. She had soft eyes, a gentle voice, and a bowl of peppermint candies wrapped in plastic on her desk to break the ice. "Tell me about what happened in the gym yesterday," she said, clicking her pen and glancing over at the clock. "Why do you think you lashed out?"

Jen shrugged, "I dunno."

Jane nodded, scribbled. "Do you ever feel like you're trying to get attention?"

Jen drops her head. "I don't know. Maybe."

Another nod. Another line scribbled on the page. Another quick check of the clock.

Jen almost broke the family rule. Mama's oldest rule: stay in character. Don't break the scene. Don't tell the truth. Even in therapy, we were still in the show.

Jen sensed Jane didn't want the script to change. And so, without a word, she fell into the part she'd been cast in. I saw her face go blank. We kept pretending. Week after week, therapy with Jane was the same routine. What did you do? Why did you do it? What coping skills could you have used instead? But never: *What hurt you? What scared you? Who was supposed to protect you and didn't?*

Jane never asked about the hospital halls where Jen learned to crawl, then walk. Never asked about Dad. Never asked what it was like to grow up with a mom who could love you and gut you in the same sentence. Maybe this was just another example of being an actor in Mama's production of illusions, showing one face and living another. No one asked why the fire was burning, just why Jen kept lighting up her life with one bad decision after another. This kept us one step away from the pain, from the truth. We learned to survive in strange ways.

Eventually, she submits to the rules. She decides to stay and do the work she needs to do to go back home to Mama instead of running. How to fold into the system just enough to survive it. She earns her privileges. Weekend furloughs. Brief trips back to Austin. Back to Mama's house. Lamar is there all the time now. He and Big Brother act like best friends. Things seem to be going well, or at least well enough that maybe things might be different with this new guy hanging around. Maybe Mama won't be so angry all the time.

At the holiday talent show, she takes center stage under hot lights in a room that smells like floor wax and cafeteria food. She sings *White Christmas* in front of staff and fellow clients into an old microphone held together with tape and time. Her voice is off-key but full of heart. And Mama comes. She even seems impressed, in that restrained kind of way. And Lamar comes. They sit in folding chairs right in the front.

For a moment she feels like someone in the right place, at the right time, doing the right thing. A rare experience for us. After the show, they meet with Jane.

"We're getting married," Mama blurts out like she forgot something at the grocery store. "We're moving. To Alabama."

Jen stares. The word "Alabama" feels like a razor-like cutting the inside of her mouth.

Lamar takes her hand in his. "We want you to come. Come with us, Darlin.'"

Mama says, "You can get your permit—you're almost 16. I'll buy you a little car."

Jane smiles at Jen like someone passing off a difficult case, "Well, you earned this."

Just like that, another door opens. A new house. A new chapter. A new self. And me? I'm still here. Watching. Guarding. Carrying it all. Because this is what we do. We don't wait for happy endings. We rebuild. Over and over.

Ruth on Gold and the Long Wait

For inner parts like me,
living in the light of awareness,
in a house where someone is truly home,
is like gold in alchemy.
Rare.
Radiant.
Holy.
It's the moment we're not just felt, but seen.
Not just tolerated, but befriended.
Cared for.
Respected.
Loved.
And for humans?
You've got your own version.
Spiritual alchemy.
The lifelong labor of turning the heavy,
stubborn lead of your mind,
your patterns, your inherited shame,

your sticky attachments,
into the gold of self-awareness.
It's not glamorous.
There's a lot of melting down involved.
The furnace gets hot.
Things bubble up.
Things burn.
It's scary shit.
It took a breakdown for Jen to find that gold.
A real one.
On-the-ground, can't-breathe, tree-whispering,
snot-on-everything kind of breakdown.
And yeah, it was awful.
But it was sacred too.
Terribly sacred.
Because down there, in the roots,
she didn't find easy answers.
She found herself.
And in finding herself,
she found the path to me.
But not all at once.
You'd think, given the importance of it all,
we'd have reunited immediately.
Nope.
That was just the spark.
The moment the crucible lit up.
Our actual relationship?
That took another decade.
That's the thing about alchemy.
The gold doesn't rush.
It takes time.
Pressure.

Tending to what most folks would rather ignore.
We came close a few times.
She tried to name me.
Wrote about me.
Researched me like I was a dissertation.
Called me her vigilance.
A sharpness.
A sense of constant alert she couldn't shake.
Can you believe that?
That's like calling your lifelong dog companion a faulty alarm clock.
But... she wasn't wrong.
Back then, I was mostly a clenched muscle.
A stomach full of diarrhea.
Sleepless nights.
Sleeping too much.
I was barking in the dark,
that she didn't know how to translate.
She thought I was the problem.
She didn't know I was the protector.
Most people don't.
That's what happens when you live too long in the wreckage—
you start thinking the smoke alarm is trying to kill you.
On some level, she always knew I was here. She felt me in a hundred different ways.
But knowing I existed isn't the same as being in a relationship with me.
And that, my friend, is gold.
Because knowing is not the same as connecting.
Thinking is not the same as listening.
Analyzing yourself isn't the same as loving your parts.

Jen analyzed our parts to pieces.
She dissected her trauma.
Charted it.
Categorized it.
Turned it into diagrams and studies.
But none of that brought her into a relationship with me.
What finally bridges that gap?
Stillness.
Listening.
Letting me speak in my own voice like here on this page.
Sharing our story from my point of view.
I didn't want to be managed.
Didn't want to be fixed, figured or footnoted.
I wanted to be known.
Felt.
Trusted.
Seen.
Touched.
Petted even.
Once she stopped trying to be one self
and opened the door to our many selves,
I could finally walk through it.
Showing myself.
Tail wagging.
Ready to help.
Turns out, I was more than her vigilance,
I was her devotion.
Her instincts.
Her pristine pattern recognition.
Her sacred knowing.
I was the dog perched at the gate of our becoming.
Standing guard until she was ready to come home.
And now?

Now we're together.
Fully. At last.
I don't have to gnaw at her guts to get her attention.
Don't need to bark into the void, hoping she'll hear me.
We sit at the same kitchen table.
She brings the tea.
I bring the tail thump.
I'm still a little bossy.
Still slightly jumpy.
But I'm not alone here anymore.
And neither is she.
Maybe that's the most beautiful thing about alchemy.
You go in thinking you'll come out shiny and whole,
but what you find is the ability to sit with your parts,
messy and brilliant and contradictory,
and say:
You too.
You belong here.
At this table.
Within me.
So if you're reading this, wondering if that voice
inside you that won't shut up
might actually be trying to help?
Listen.
Not with your ears.
With your presence.
With your heart.
There's gold inside your house too.
Buried beneath the wreckage.
Waiting in the dust.
Glinting softly in the dark.

—*Ruth*

Chapter 4:

Stitching

Jen — Winter 2022

Every morning before leaving the hotel, I follow the same quiet ritual. Not because I *have* to, but because I *want* to. Ritual and routine feel good in my soul, but it definitely wasn't always this way.

I get Frannie settled: her favorite blanket, entertainment cued up, snacks arranged in order by time. The pups curl into their usual spots, already learning the rhythm of our strange new life. There's a quietness to our mornings that feels both sacred and practical.

I grab a slice of bread, sourdough if I can get it, spread it with olive oil butter, and wrap it in a paper towel. I don't usually eat this early, but I need the energy.

Clean boots and a piece of bread count as morning prayers.

First thing I see when I get up? My red boots are smiling at me. I scrub them in the hotel bathtub every night. It takes effort, my body burns from the day of working, every joint protesting as I lower myself down far enough to reach the faucet, to turn the water on, to kneel beside the tub. I always worry that I won't be able to get back up. Sometimes it happens. But usually Iris is nearby. She's not here though. By the end of the day every move feels as dramatic as a hostage negotiation. I wash away layers of Mama's house—layers of dust, dirt, old grief. The water in the tub turns dark gray, then brown, then clear. I love that kind of alchemy. I dry the boots with the same hotel towel and leave them by the door. Somehow, the doing of it, the choice to show up for this small act of care, reminds me who I am. Not just what I'm surviving, and what I have survived, but who I've always been, who I am and who I am becoming.

Somehow, seeing them there in the morning helps me. They're waiting. Steady. Patient.

It's like they're saying, *"We're with you. Let's go…"*

The hotel staff has been kind, offering us the hospital rate during the week now that Iris' points have run out. On weekends, we pay full price. Today, the place is crawling with glitter-dusted cheerleaders and their moms. Almost no one is masked. That worries me because if I catch Covid, that could spell disaster for Mama. I slip stealthily through the high-pitched giggles wandering together in gaggles, masked and cautious, past the chaos of the lobby that's too bright. The whole hotel is lit up by fluorescent lights, too loud, too early.

I make my way to the quiet, dark underground parking garage below the hotel where Mama's car waits: a brand-new

Kia Soul Iris and I helped her buy it a few months ago. Her first brand new car. It's become my chariot now. I press the clicker, and the lights flash. A small sound in a giant concrete cavern.

That's when I hear them: birds. Tucked somewhere overhead in the concrete rafters, singing. Their songs are sharp and indignant. They've built nests in the beams overhead and raised generations of babies in this fume-filled cave of car exhaust and echoes of people coming and going.

We make homes where we can.
We work with what we've got.
And when we're lucky—we sing.

I pause beside the car to wish the birds overhead a good day. I think they wish me one too.

Driving through Huntsville, I spot them again, pigeons lined up like music notes on a wire, still but watching. Friends. I've always felt them as earthbound angels. On hard days. On magical ones. They were there the day I got out of jail, when Mama picked me up, unsmiling, silent. But she came. They were there when Iris took me for Thai food on her first visit to Huntsville. I remember when her hand brushed mine at the table like it was no big deal but it felt like the biggest deal in the world.

Pigeons on power lines are my own small crowd of witnesses. A whole community cheering me on. Encouraging me to stay. Running away from this town won't save me, I have to face it. All of it, Mama, the mess, the memories, the truth. The only way through...is through. And I've got friends, feathered friends, loyal, seen and unseen, to get me through this. Mama's life depends on it.

We're good in hard times.

She's right, we are.

It's warmer today, so I leave the space heaters off. I still don't trust that ancient fuse box powering mama's house. I text a photo of the electrical panel to a local guy, but he didn't reply. That worries me. The new HVAC install is scheduled for next week.

I let the dogs out, two by two, on leashes. Refill food and water bowls. Clean up a hallway of turds nestled on old towels. Feed Hong Hua, Mama's red betta fish. Willy, a pota-to-shaped dog that was initially shy, trusts me enough now that he insists on being carried everywhere. He gets special wet food. Ruth and I honor his fiery trust. We know what it means to be cautious survivors. These dogs are grieving and I'm no substitute for Mama, their pack leader, their heartbeat.

I can't imagine being cut off from you again.

That's never gonna happen.

The nurse calls and says Mama might be discharged tomorrow. She's kept down a few sips of Ensure, and even has strength to text me that she only wants the strawberry kind.

Gotta find the strawberry kind...

I wash Mama's well-worn bedding, fold her red flannel nightgown, wipe down and arrange her bedside table with her glasses, tissues, meds, and the remote control. I line up clean puke buckets. Her homecoming feels real. Imminent.

Next on my list: the untouched room. Mama and Lamar's bedroom. She hasn't set foot there since he died. Says it's too dark. She's not wrong. It's a time capsule sealed in grief, draped in thick dust and the most epic spider webs I've ever seen. Once a sanctuary. Now a spider shrine.

The furniture is heavy, not just in weight but in memories. A matched set in bright blonde wood: a bed, nightstands, towering hutch, all weirdly glowing beneath a thick veil of neglect. Mama used to spend hours here, flipping through daylily catalogs under that awful overhead fluorescent light. Stacks of magazines still sit on the nightstand, dog-eared and marked up in highlighter—her latest flower finds for the gardens they once dreamed of, built, and took care of together. *Dreamscape Gardens*, they called it.

Lamar—gentle, blue-eyed Lamar. He loved Mama with every cell in his body. She loved him the same. Their bond was primal. Animal-deep. He was her one true mate for life. Her only safe place.

His death unmoored her. Alzheimer's took his mind. Cancer took the rest. She stayed through it all—every brutal day—holding his hand as he slipped away. After that, she let the whole house swallow her alive. She became a ghost, yet still very much alive.

Inside their old room, the spider webs are wild, like something out of a dream or a prayer.

Threads stretch from corner to corner, cascading from the ceiling fan like lace. The mirror is veiled in silk, strands glistening like Indra's Net. A web lost to time. A meditation on loss. Almost too beautiful to destroy. But I can't let them stay. This house is gonna live again.

I spray peppermint oil cleaner in every direction, turning the room into a candy cane death trap. That just pisses them off. The spiders dig in. Doubling down.

Ruth has a better idea: *Be who you need to be. This is sacred work.*

Just like that I transform into Kali: the goddess of sacred demolition. Yellow gloves. Red boots. Shop Vac in hand. I have become more than human. Three hours later, my body burns. My spine is screaming. But I've cleared every corner.

Offering apologies to the spiders the whole time, "I'm sorry. Forgive me. Shit. I'm really sorry."

It's a strange mix of grief and purpose. The paradox is real! That's how I know I'm on the right path, whenever paradox shows up.

I dump the vacuum canister out in the field far from the house. Maybe some spiders will rebuild. Somewhere safer. Away from Kali and her shop-vac of destruction. In some traditions, spiders are good luck. I've just vacuumed entire civilizations and generations of them. Maybe not my luckiest day.

Or maybe it is? Life never arrives in clean packages. It's always a mixed bag of bad luck and good luck. Sometimes, sacred work looks like vacuuming spider cathedrals in someone else's forgotten room..

Exhausted, I take a break and check GoFundMe. Donations are still coming in, one miracle at a time.

Mama's coming home to a safer place than she left. There's so much still to do—but this house feels different. Lighter. It breathes again as I catch my own breath.

Later I visit Mama at the hospital. She stirs, but doesn't want anything to do with me. That's a longstanding vibe between her and I. "Don't turn on the lights," she commands, like she did back when she was a Sergeant in the Marines.

Darkness is her cocoon. Familiar. Safe.

Back at the hotel, the ritual is the same: Take care of my pack, clean my boots. Shower. Collapse into bed like the crumpled to-do list in my pocket and my mind.

The next morning, I'm back at it. I get to Mama's house to take the dogs out, then drive over the mountain to pick her up from the hospital. I corner the nurse working on her discharge paperwork.

"She wasn't like this before surgery. Why is she like this now?" The nurse shrugs. Offers no satisfying answers, only repeating the suggestion to reach out to the surgeon. The stomach pain. Nausea. Weight loss—it doesn't add up. We need answers. But we take the meds and accept the discharge. I'm just glad she's getting out of here alive.

At home, the dogs lose their minds with joy. They bark loudly, dance in circles, leap up to kiss her hands like she's the queen returning to her castle. Their love is loud and unquestioning. No hesitation. No restraint.

Mama steps over them with practiced ease, barely acknowledging the commotion. She makes a beeline to her bedroom and shuts the door. It's all too much.

I don't blame her. The house has changed. The light moves differently now. The air's been stirred. I'm relieved she doesn't notice the specifics yet. But I know she knows. She can feel it.

She may not say it. She may never say it. But her silence holds weight. She knows I've been working on things. And for now, that's enough.

She sips electrolyte water from a plastic bottle in bed, her hands a little shaky but steady enough to hold it. I keep a close eye on her, watching for signs. Breath. Color. Strength.

She eats a few bites of instant mashed potatoes I've microwaved in a bowl with faded green leaves on the rim. That's all she wants. I added a little butter so they wouldn't crust over on top, so they'd feel more like food. It's something. Maybe not a feast. But it's warm. It's salt. It's a kind of love.

Her longtime friend Liz lives close by and agrees to be on call while I return to the hotel for the night to care for Frannie and the pups.

"Thank you," I say. "If Mama needs anything..."

"Of course," Liz says. "Anything."

That one word—*anything*—lands soft on my shoulders. Not everything. Not a fix. But something.

Mama lets the dogs pile into bed with her. A circle of devotion. Fur pressed to skin. Paws draped across legs. They don't know she's fragile. They only know she's home. She's held. In presence. In paws. In this broken house held together by duct tape. She's safe for tonight.

Thursday comes and I keep cleaning. Each step is a blessing. Each scrub a hallelujah. Mama's up. Awake in bed playing solitaire on her tablet tapping softly. Spa music hums from the TV like a distant lullaby. She's sipping tea. Not puking.

All great signs.

We're not done. But we're coming through this. One step at a time.

The junk haulers arrive. Three kind men. They haul away furniture, trash, and the broken fridge. The rooms exhale. The house exhales. So do we.

Mama says the fence idea is smart. Her voice is quiet, but sure.

"Lamar and I talked about it," she says, eyes distant. "Just never happened."

I nod. I don't press. There's a whole lot that never happened. So many things that only saw light in the talking stage.

But this, this is happening. Posts are going in the ground. A real fence. Real protection. A little ease to an uneasy situation.

I feel Lamar everywhere. In the corners of the house. In the slant of afternoon sunlight across the linoleum he and I picked out together so many years ago. I imagine him beaming at the work we've done, smiling that Hollywood smile at the slow resurrection of their house, at the way I've returned not just to clean things up, but to care for Mama. To love the house into repair.

I believe he'd be proud. Not just of our progress, but the heart behind it. I imagine tomorrow, when Iris comes back, she'll beam at me a lot like Lamar did. That same quiet faith. That same look that says, *I see you.* Unconditional love. Unyielding support. Not loud, not performative. Just...true. The kind of love that stays no matter what.

My kind of love.

The winter weather is wild. Sun, wind, snow. Then sun again. I text Liz and ask her to be on call just in case Mama needs anything. Back at the hotel, I start my nightly ritual. Boots. Shower. Check-in. Collapse.

On Friday I clean the yard, clear a space for the new fence. Mama's plant collection—hibernating in their pots—waits for spring. This house is her sanctuary. Broken as it is, it's her happy place. Her safe place where she lived with her only safe person. Sometimes safe places don't look like we expect them to. I appreciate that more than ever as I watch her move around the yard. Mama waters plants from a coffee mug. Eats more microwave potatoes. All signs that she's healing.

I think we're heading in the right direction...

The fence team arrives on time. By afternoon, the yard is wrapped in a sparkling silver hug. "Come see your new fence," I pop my head into her room with a big smile.

She steps into the backyard in her red plaid flannel nightgown, feet snug in thick socks and sherpa-lined Crocs. Beaming. Mama rarely smiles like that. I snap a photo, then open the back door, the dogs rush out like kids at recess. Joy, unleashed.

Mama and her pack return to bed not long after. Progress.

Then gravel arrives, piled high in the driveway to fill potholes. Another gift from The Roberts Family.

Ruth reminds me—*Text Nina's landscaper.*

Then finally: Iris arrives. Relief floods me. I show her everything. The rooms. The fence. All my work. Part of me is sure she's gonna be mad at me for working hard and doing so much. "It's beautiful," she says. No judgment. Just love.

We leave Mama settled and return to the hotel for the night. The shift is immediate. The air is lighter, the silence is ours. A different kind of tiredness sets in.

After a shower, I fill the tub for my boots. I scrub them gently, slowly, like a closing ritual—washing off the film of the day, the ache of the house, the memory of spiders. I'm so glad to be on the other side of this ordeal.

We put on sweats. Frannie's in PJs, hair wet from a bath. Her feet shuffle against the carpet, soft and familiar.

Then: tornado warnings. We check the radar—spirals of red and orange lines are sweeping toward us.

Yikes.

We call the front desk. They tell us to come downstairs, the banquet room is safest.

We pack light. Put a leash on Pax, and wrap Wicky in a blanket like a burrito. I tuck him against my chest. We grab Wion, of course, Wicky's stuffed ragged lion soulmate rides in Frannie's arms like our family talisman.

Downstairs, the banquet room has transformed into a makeshift shelter. No windows. Just dim lights and a weird hush over the space like a collective breath is being held in there.

We pick a table and settle near the wall. Other families start to join us, some with dogs, others with kids clinging to tablets. Frannie plugs into hers. Iris scans for exits, instinctively. She's just as vigilant as we are. We love that about her. One of a million things.

Ruth hums low in my bones—*good job, pack leader.*

We wait out the storm. No one seems panicked, but no one's relaxed either.

Eventually, the radar clears. The warnings lift. We rise together, one small pod, grateful and intact. As we leave the banquet room, we pass a group of families still camped out under the three story high glass ceiling in the atrium. They're happily watching football on a giant screen.

Ruth and I glance at each other inwardly, and say it at the same time, that's the last place we'd be in a storm. Under a glass ceiling! We lived through too many rooms like that. Ones that looked safe from the outside, but shattered the moment the slightest pressure hit. We know better now. We move differently than most folks.

Back upstairs in our room, we crawl into bed. Dogs pile in. Frannie tucks into bed. Iris is warm next to me. We sleep soundly. It's good to be together again.

Saturday morning Iris and Frannie head to Starbucks, Frannie's reward for being so good all week. She's been a trooper. I stay behind, sit in the quiet. Let the stillness wrap around me, just for a moment. No shop-vac screaming. Dogs barking. No nagging to-do list in my hand. Just me, Ruth, and our circle of selves reflecting on everything we've moved through.

This week has been a vortex of ups and downs, spiraling between despair and delight, pain and progress, collapse and connection. Mama's house. Mama's body. My body. Our hearts each battered in their own ways, all working together to pull off the impossible. Not perfection. Not a resolution. Just progress.

We're almost there.

When they return, I thank them. "Couldn't do all this without you guys. Love you both."

Iris and I go back to Mama's to tackle the garage. Lamar's sacred space. We open the heavy door, and the air shifts, cooler, denser. His tools are still there, exactly where he left them. Covered in dusty webs, rust along the handles. His candle molds, once carefully stored on makeshift shelves, have collapsed with time. Some bent. Some cracked.

A mad mix of scents still clings to the air—wax, dust, cedar, a trace of honeysuckle. It's like walking into a candle store that's been forgotten by time. He used to make candles for the winter luminary display on Monte Sano mountain. Hundreds of luminaries, each one poured by hand, set to cool in quiet rows. We learned all about candle making right after Mama and Lamar got married. We rolled the freshly poured candles, one by one, along old rags to round out their square edges, softening them with each pass. Slipping wicks into carefully drilled holes in the center. Laughing together.

Lamar was patient with us. Gentle. He was our light in every way. Now, all these years later, I wanna reclaim it. Not just reclaim the physical space—but the warmth and the light.

Mama peeks in. Doesn't say a word. Just nods with that stern look of approval only she can make, tight-lipped, slightly suspicious, unmistakably Mama. For her, this is permission. For us, it's a green light to keep going

Later that night, we left Mama early, she seems to be doing great. We reward Frannie by ordering dinner to be delivered to the hotel, her choice tonight.

Settling in for the night, I finally let myself exhale. The dogs are fed. Frannie's tucked in. Iris is brushing her teeth. Then, my phone rings.

"Mama?" Her voice is small, strained, stranded. "Jen, I need to go back to the hospital. My stomach. I'm cold. Something's not right."

My heart lurches into motion before the rest of me does.

"Hold on," I say, already moving. "I'm coming."

I grab the keys. Ruth and I move like greased lightning—not in speed, but in clarity. Everything is sharp. Everything focused.

The pain in my body screams, but there's no time to negotiate with it right now. I slide behind the wheel, fly over the mountain, and haul ass down the highway. I'm pretty certain I'm about to get a speeding ticket. But I don't care. All I care about is Mama.

Ruth hums steady in my bones: *Keep going. Stay sharp. She needs you.*

Then, like something out of a movie! A deputy is parked on the median, right in front of her house on the highway. Miraculously placed. Almost as if he was waiting for me. I flash my headlights—once, twice. Shimmy my car right up beside his patrol vehicle in a bold move I'm pretty sure he didn't appreciate. I roll down my window and yell with everything I've got:

"That's my Mama's house. She's sick. I need help."

There's a pause—brief but loaded. The kind of pause where fate decides what happens next.

My hand grips the steering wheel like a lifeline. Ruth's right at my throat, ears up, pulse hot.

This is the moment it could go sideways. Be misread. Be nothing but a woman shouting into the night air.

But then, the deputy nods, shifts his car into gear and follows as I race across the road into Mama's gravel driveway.

I find her inside, hunched over, heaving. I help her out of the house by myself, and we meet the deputy outside. He's already radioed for an ambulance, they're on their way.

And we wait, just the three of us in Mama's driveway, lit by his headlights, a dark night of the soul made brighter by this stranger's care.

Then the strangest thing happened. His radio crackled to life. The dispatcher's voice comes through, matter-of-fact, dry as dust:"10-95 responding to domestic disturbance. Be advised: a deer is living in the residence."

The deputy and I looked at each other, caught in the same question–did we just hear that right? A deer. Living inside someone's house. We didn't say a word. Just stood there, two lizards stuck in an Alabama blizzard, blinking at the wildness of it all. Nothing and everything makes sense right now.

The ambulance arrives, and the paramedics are kind with Mama, they lift her with care.

"I'll watch the house tonight," the deputy says. "I'm out here patrolling this strip of the highway."

"Thank you," I say. "We're so lucky you were here when we needed you..."

He nods. "Sometimes life just lines up that way."

And it really, truly does.

Ruth — 1988

*S*ome homes are rebuilt with lumber and nails. Others with survival, sheer will, and memories. Jen is doing both. She's laying down gravel and prayers, vacuuming up spiderwebs and ancestral wounds. She's rebuilding a house—and herself—from the bones up. That's the real work of healing, isn't it? Letting the breath return to places that forgot how to breathe.

No structure repairs itself without first revealing where it cracked. So we go back. To the blueprints that shaped her. To the years that taught her who and who not to become. To the young woman who learned to armor herself to survive. The house remembers. And so do I.

For Mama, married life with Lamar is everything she ever dreamed of—and everything she deserves. He dotes on her with a kindness that softens her edges, slightly. Together they build a quiet life around the things that bring her joy: dogs, cats, plants, and hard-won peace. Big Brother joins the military soon after the move, and the house settles into a slower rhythm.

For Jen, Alabama feels like exile. She's fifteen. Loud.

Smart. Wild. A streetwise city kid dropped into a town with no sidewalks and a Piggly Wiggly that still has carpet. She aches for the chaos of Austin—for late-night buses and friends who tripped on LSD.

She tries her best to play the part of the good daughter, the one she imagined she'd be while back at Waco Center for Youth, a good girl in tenth grade at New Hope High—how poetic. The cracks show up fast. She's partying. Sneaking out of the house. Forging checks to buy her way into friend groups with gifts. When Mama finds the stolen checks, she doesn't have Jen arrested. She covers for her at the small-town bank, and then delivers a verbal ass-whooping so sharp it leaves bruises on the soul that never heal. Mama never hit with hands. Her words landed harder than anything.

School for Jen isn't much better. In science class, a teacher tells Jen to spit out her gum or go to the principal's office. She blows a huge bubble, pops it, and walks out with a smirk. "Fine by me." She never did take kindly to being told what to do. Mama hated that about her, and Jen took that as a challenge. She lives on her own terms.

Then there's Milly. A friend with a car, which means freedom. Mama said Jen didn't deserve that car she promised when they moved from Texas after stealing those checks. Milly's car offers more than rides, it becomes an escape hatch from small town Alabama.

They cruise into Huntsville, windows down, up over the mountain, cassette tapes blaring *Push It*, by Salt-N-Pepa, shoulders move back and forth, feet tapping, wind tangled hair. It's far enough to feel like they're leaving everything behind, they stay out long enough to pretend they could.

Milly is dating a soldier at Redstone Arsenal, a military base in Huntsville. Just through basic training, he's a young guy sporting a sharp buzz-cut, swagger, and confidence for days. He sneaks off base when he can. Makes Milly feel like she's doing something wild and grown up.

One night, Milly calls Jen: "You wanna come with? He's bringing a friend named Matt."

Matt is twenty-one. Baby-faced. Sweet. Blue eyes like Lamar's, only younger, a little cooler. He calls her pretty. Offers her his high school letterman's jacket even though it's barely cold. He doesn't flinch when she talks too much or goes quiet for too long. It's like he sees her.

Jen falls fast. Not because they're soulmates. But because they're both starving. Starving for attention. For escape. For affection that isn't laced with judgment. For anything that feels like love, even if it's just the outline of it. Jen figures she can color in the details later.

By their fourth hangout, they're tangled up in the back of Milly's car, and Matt whispers:

"If your mom signs, we can get married."

Jen doesn't hesitate. At sixteen, she drops out of New Hope High and becomes his wife.

Mama is resigned, oddly relieved. Without Jen there it's a lot easier to make her dreams come true with Lamar. She makes Jen promise to get her GED. She even buys her a navy blue Gunny Sax dress—floral print, puffy sleeves, and lace, a little too modest and childishly innocent for the occasion, but exactly right for a teenager trying to become a woman overnight.

The wedding ceremony is in Florida at Matt's family home. No church. No aisle. Just a collection of chairs in his house flanked by a bunch of relatives Jen's never met. His mom is nice to Jen, but his sisters are suspicious of her.

Lamar and Mama don't come but they do make good on

that promise Mama made and give the couple a used car as a wedding present, and send them on their way to Oklahoma where Matt is newly stationed. The ride is awkward. Tender. Passionate. Hopeful. For a brief flicker of time, it feels good, like a new beginning. Underneath their wedding vows and her child-woman dress, fragile fault lines appear.

Love doesn't pay the bills. A private's salary barely covers gas, much less rent or food. Jen's underage, and Matt's commanding officer keeps demanding that she go back to Alabama even though they are legally married. That only makes her more determined to stay.

Jen's anger doesn't simmer, it boils over. Fights with Matt are sharp. Explosive. Loud enough to rattle the windows.

She yells. Slams cabinet doors. Stomps out of rooms barefoot, crying, out of control, daring him to follow. Sometimes she throws things, not to hurt, but to shatter the silence that always follows his inaction.

His silence feels like betrayal. Matt won't stand up for her. Won't even stand up for himself. Not when the guys in his unit make jokes about her age. Not when they talk trash behind his back. They call him Sad Sack, over and over, like it's funny. He just shrugs. Laughs it off. Like it's easier to accept his fate than to defend his honor.

But Jen didn't get married to disappear. To be quiet. She got married to be *chosen*. To be fought for. She's never been fond of sad sacks. Never trusted people who fold before they're even hit. She's spent her whole life clawing her way into spaces that didn't want her, always speaking up, even when her voice shook. She can't respect a man whose main magic trick is vanishing in plain sight.

And so she yells. And yells. Because he won't. The more he won't, the more she does. Enough for two people.

The marriage dissolves within a year. No dramatic final straw, just the slow, painful erosion of everything Jen hoped it could be. Too many silences. Too much shrinking. It wasn't just that he wouldn't fight back, it was the way he disappeared like fog slipping under the door. He left first. Maybe not actually but, in every way that mattered to her.

She files for divorce. Refuses to go back to Alabama, to the place where she never felt like she fit in anyway. And the last thing she wants is Mama calling the shots again. Instead, she finds a place of her own. A tiny house near the Army base, barely big enough for her giant waterbed, a table, and a secondhand dresser with sticky drawers. But it's hers.

To survive, she takes a job at the Post Exchange—cashing checks behind bulletproof glass. It pays just enough to scrape by. Rent. Gas. Boxed mac and cheese. She gets good at the rhythm of it. Smiles on cue. Counts fast. A pen behind each ear. Jen likes people. Enjoys the parade of faces and stories. Soldiers and spouses. Mothers with toddlers. The most important thing is the feeling that she is in charge of her destiny.

Then one day—*he walks in.* Captain Brice Allen Peterson. Dress blues. Chest full of ribbons. A smile too big for the room. He walks around like he owns the space around him.

"Hey good lookin', whatcha got cookin'?" he says, grinning like a game show host. His moves are bold. Jen can't breathe. His voice was shaped like a blade, smooth enough to draw you in, sharp enough to leave a permanent scar. She doesn't even register his words. Just stares at those big flawless teeth, so polished, so perfect, so weaponized for charm. His eyes beam like searchlights on the prowl. Jen loves his attention.

He keeps coming back to cash checks. Always waits in

her line. Same crooked smile. Flirting like it's a sport he always wins. Seductive. Dangerous. Magnetic in that irresistible way, almost like cutting her own skin always made her feel in control. Real.

She writes down the address on his check. Can't help herself. Something reckless lights up inside. Not just curiosity. Not a dare. A flicker of *what if* and *why not me*. A hunger she can't name, but doesn't want to quiet. She's hungry to be seen. Hungry to be wanted. To rewrite the story of herself, fast, messy, loud.

On her day off, she drives to his apartment complex, a place with an ugly concrete courtyard with peeling paint and rusted metal pool furniture. She gets out and circles the courtyard once. Twice. Hoping for a little dumb luck.

And there he is. At the top of the stairs, arms spread like he'd been waiting for her all along.

"Hey! It's you! I know you!" he says like it's fate. Like the whole thing was meant to be.

That's all it takes. It happens on her nineteenth birthday. After a whirlwind romance, they elope at the courthouse in a flash of impulse and imagined safety, chasing something that felt like fate. No dress, no bouquet, no witnesses. Just a swishy skirt, chipped nail polish, and bright pink lip gloss she applies and reapplies like body armor. Brice, starched and proud in his dress blues, holds her close with a grip that feels like devotion. He calls her his wife loud enough for the whole world to hear. She loves that.

At the officers' club, everything gleams, polished floors, polished ranks, polished people. The kind of place where everyone knows everyone. Jen walks in like she belongs. Like she was always meant to be there. She's arm-in-arm with her new husband, but she carries herself.

Then, we see him. That same commanding officer from before. The one who looked her up and down and told her "go back to Alabama" when she was married to Matt, like she was a temporary inconvenience. Like she was a kid with too many feelings and not enough use.

As he sees her, something flickers in his eyes. A recognition. Jen doesn't blink. Her chin lifts. Her mouth curves, just slightly, into something that might've been a smile. She looks right at him, full Peer stare. Maybe a challenge. Not smug. Not spiteful. Just...certain she's in the right place. She's back in her power. And for a second, I believe it too.

Brice's arm tightens around her arm, not gently, not sweet. Like he owns her. I watched the way she glanced up at him, wondering if maybe he saw what she saw in that moment. Maybe he'll celebrate with her, this moment of feeling alive in her own skin. He doesn't. He's too busy soaking in the attention. Too busy showing her off like some prize he won, not like someone he loves. I file it away. That grip. The glance. His absence of celebration.

One segment on the local news broadcast in this part of Oklahoma was called Waiting Child. Every week, they'd air a short clip of a kid in foster care looking for a family to adopt them. Sometimes siblings were featured. There was gentle theme music that settled in your heart and stayed there. Then came the interview: A lady asking soft questions, a child giving answers. A sweet, smiling face being extra cute for the camera. If the music didn't grab her heartstrings, those innocent eyes sure did.

So many kids needed a family. Jen studied those TV segments closely, daydreamed about what it would be like if one of those kids were hers. She knew she couldn't have children in the usual way. That door had been shut by the radiation they used to save her life when she was the size of a loaf of bread. All those Waiting Child segments woke up something in her, turned her heart into a magnet for a kid. She became single-mindedly focused on becoming a mom. Making a family. Brice went along with it, not enthusiastically. He wanted a child from his bloodline, something Jen couldn't give.

The idea of loving someone else's child as her own made perfect sense. Heart sense. At a foster care information event where prospective parents have the chance to get to know available foster kids, Jen sees a grainy VCR recording playing on a TV. There on the screen was Frannie—our small, skinny, sweet moon-faced kid swallowed up in clothes way too big. Not looking directly at the camera, but through it. As if she was waiting for someone to show up. Jen was drawn to that screen without hesitation. She didn't know her name yet. Didn't know the whole story. Didn't understand the gravity of what they were stepping into. But she said it out loud anyway, clear, and confident as the day is long. "That one," she said. "We'll help her."

The social worker, a nice lady named Lynette, said this might be Frannie's last chance at living in a home with a family, of possibily getting adopted. Her next stop was likely to be a long term residential facility after a string of failed foster care placements and violent, unpredictable outbursts. Jen and Brice look over the reports, see a handful of family photos, and try to comprehend the disturbing details about everything Frannie survived in her short few years of life. Brice and Jen say yes to the placement before even meeting her.

Frannie was a six year old feral kid everyone had discarded. Not feral in a bad way, feral as in never given any meaningful stability or care. She was born with Fetal

Hydantoin Syndrome, her mom overdosed on seizure medicine at some point while pregnant. The report said she was trying to kill herself. But life had other plans. Frannie was born into a nightmare, her nervous system was shattered before she ever had a chance to feel safe in it. Abused. Betrayed. Abandoned. Unwanted. Relinquished to the state. Sunk into foster care. She was on her way to being institutionalized.

It makes no sense to adopt this kid so soon after getting married to a guy she hardly knows, but Jen insists to everyone it's a soul-knowing. A body-deep call to action. Brice goes along with her plan, maybe out of compassion, but mostly because it gives Jen something to do. Something to focus on. Plus it makes him look good. His rank in the military gives them an air of stability, order, and responsibility. On paper, they're the perfect couple, an officer and his bright, determined young wife.

Brice and Jen complete many hours of foster care training together. Lynette the social worker visits their place. They pass the home study with flying colors after cleaning meticulously, answering questions with rehearsed answers, smiling on cue. The state of Oklahoma buys it.

Foster placement is granted. The first thing Frannie does when she arrives at her new home is march into the front yard, drop her pants in full view of a family of welcoming neighbors, and pees on the grass. She was six years old. No one had taught her any different.

Jen's undeterred by the behavior, and within months the adoption is finalized. Just like that, Frannie becomes their legal daughter. Of course, nothing about this situation is simple. Jen doesn't step into motherhood with ease. She steps in with fire. With instinct. With reckless abandon. With loyalty born from knowing what it feels like to be left alone.

Frannie doesn't arrive soft and graceful. She's wild. Guarded. Angry. Fluent in the language of survival. Jen sees through that, she speaks the same language of survival. Recognizes the spark in Frannie's eyes, the magic in her, the incredible force of her sheer will to survive. She chooses a child who reflects her sense of self: Unwanted. Undeniably worthy. Impossible to love. Impossible not to love.

Paper-thin promises can't meet the needs of a traumatized child. And Brice? He's a cheater. A liar. A man who left a trail of damage behind him like the thick smoke from his chain of cigarettes. Jen was clinging to promises he never meant to keep. But even in this wreckage, a miracle took root, this is how Jen became Frannie's mom.

Their marriage collapses under the weight of broken commitments. But Jen won't break her promise to Frannie. Not ever. She won't be another person discarding her precious life. Brice files for divorce and denies any paternity. Mama's livid by that ballsy move, she drains her savings to pay for the best lawyer she can afford, who provides proof of the adoption to the court.

In 1994, Jen returned to Alabama. Not as a girl, as a woman-child with a whole lotta scars. Twenty-one going on fifty-five. Jen and Frannie move into a small apartment, just far enough from Mama and Lamar for independence, close enough to reach for help. Money is tight. Rent is due. No child support. No job. No childcare. No good options. Frannie is volatile. She screams. Breaks things. Most people don't last ten minutes in a room with her.

The apartment was cramped, two-bedrooms, one bathroom. It smelled like ramen noodles and restless nights. The walls were thin, the fridge rattled, and the sharp scent of anxiety hung low in the air of our lives.

Frannie had intense storms inside. Jen could feel them coming, the sky would grow dark across the apartment, she'd get tight in her eyes, there was a weird flickering in her little fingers. She didn't know how to say what was wrong, not in words anyway. Not yet, so Frannie screamed those feelings with her whole body.

There were juice boxes hurled across the kitchen like they had betrayed her. Then the dolls. She tore their heads off with precision, not cruelty. Poked their eyeballs with anything sharp, "Bad baby!" Like she was interrupting some nightmare mid-sentence. Her body would jerk to a stop, then she'd go completely still. I watched Frannie go somewhere else, eyes locked on air, she was tracking something no one else could see. Then, it came. Full on rage. Desperate, wordless groans. Her own language. She spun round and round in endless circles. Started throwing whatever she could grab. Forks. Shoes. Bowls from the sink.

Jen never retreated, she moved closer. Crouched low. I was there, watching from the corner. Professionals labeled it behavioral problems. Oppositional Defiant Disorder. Said Frannie was damaged beyond repair. I knew better. There was brilliance underneath those storms. Her body was metabolizing grief, abuse, confusion, all the horrible experiences she'd been through before she came to Jen. Trauma spoke through her hands, through silence, through random objects flying across that tiny apartment.

Jen? She was still a kid practically. Trying to be a mom without a model. Extinguishing wildfires she didn't set with nothing more than a damp washcloth in her hands. She never stopped trying. She held on. Held onto Frannie best she could. Dodged what she had to.

One night, the neighbor, Pam, knocked. She'd heard something through the wall, probably noticed the exhaustion written in Jen's eyes. Said she'd be happy to stay with Frannie at night if Jen ever needed a sitter. "She's a deep sleeper, right?" Pam asked, gentle but firm. "I'll be right next door."

Jen scans the classifieds, hoping something, anything, might appear. Night work. Some way to make money. With a GED, who is going to hire her?

An ad on the page blinks like a neon omen: **Want to make great cash? Work at night? Outgoing? DANCERS WANTED!! No experience necessary. Ask for Bub.**

She impulsively rips it from the paper. But then, hesitates. What would she even wear? What do strippers wear?

She digs out a tight black dress from that Halloween party with Brice. It used to make her feel sexy. He told her it made her look fuckable. Now it just makes her feel seen. Exactly what she needs.

Then she remembers the corset. Black satin. Lace-up. A new kind of armor. Perfect for hiding the scars and lopsided belly she never shows anyone. She tears through boxes until she finds it. Holds it to her chest like a promise.

It wasn't a promise. I knew that. She couldn't hear me back then. I went from inner voice, to way back in the shadow. From shadow to barely a scent. I stayed close in whatever form she'd let me.

The next night, she feeds Frannie dinner. Tucks her in. Waits for Pam to arrive. Then drives off to Jimmy's Lounge.

A blinking sign floods the car in pulses of light and dark. We're on high alert. But Jen? She's resolute. She watches the parade of women and men coming and going. Takes a breath.

She keeps choosing numbness. She will walk in. She will dance. She will earn what's needed. Not because she wants to. But because she thinks she has to. Because she's fluent in survival. Because she's willing to do whatever it takes. Willing to go too far for all the right reasons. Even if it means dancing under the dim lights in a strip club out on the edge of nowhere Alabama. Even if it means being someone else to be herself.

She believes she was built for this. She's been rehearsing and shape-shifting her whole life. I've been with her every step of the way, guardian, mapmaker, her loyal dog underneath the table where she dances for strangers, keeping watch while she builds rooms out of endless disappointment.

Chapter 5:

Rooting

Jen — Winter 2022

Mama's readmitted to the hospital for the same reasons as before: intractable vomiting, abdominal pain, uncontrollable chills, fever. When I visit, she's asleep—knocked out by morphine, her face curled towards the wall. The room is dark, though it's midday. Through the shade, I can just make out the view of Huntsville nestled in the valley of Monte Sano, Spanish for Mountain of Health.

This town was built on the promise of healing. People came here for the clean air and mineral springs, hoping to cure diphtheria, yellow fever, tuberculosis. Monte Sano even had a luxury health resort back in the 1800s. A healing place.

I used to escape up to the mountain. Sleep in a hammock

between trees, zip myself up into a tent. Sometimes with friends. Usually with weed. Sometimes I tripped on LSD underneath the trees and felt like I was dissolving into bark, moon, and sky. I dated a woman who lived in a tiny stone house up there. Most times, I just drove. Flying down the mountain's sharp curves too fast, tempting fate, not because I wanted to die. I just wanted *distance* from the one thing I couldn't outrun: being me.

I didn't care for that.

I know. I'm sorry. I was lost. Until we were found.

Yep, we were found.

It's always been that way. The mountain rising above it all, full of history and memories, cloaked in the passing seasons in gold, green, silver, and then icy white and bare. Dangerous. There's nothing more edgy than driving up, across, and then down those tight bends of Monte Sano when it's frozen.

When I met Iris, I couldn't wait to bring her up there. Still in my wheelchair after pelvic fusion surgery, she helped me transfer with a board to my wheelchair, and gently, patiently, wheeled me out to the bluff. We were giddy. Silly. So high on the mountain, on each other., on the gold and green mountain ranges below us, stacked like sleeping bodies.

She proposed a few years later, I walked right out to that same bluff on my own two feet. Her love delivered me to better health, not just in my body, but in my spirit, in my mind and soul. She loved me in places that didn't know what it was to be held with warmth and care.

Here I am again. Not on a bluff, but out on an edge no less, in this cold hospital room with the sound of the slow beeps tracking Mama's heart. She's still asleep. Monte Sano shimmers in the background, just out of reach. A healing place, once. And maybe, if we can get through this, again.

The nurse comes in the room with her computer attached to a rolling cart, interrupting our walk down memory lane. Her voice is thick as southern butter biscuits. "Yer mom's gettin' a feedin' tube. TPN. It'll go straight in her veins. She's losin' too much weight."

"Will she need it long term?"

She stops typing, sharpens her eyes at me, the only point of her face I can see because of her mask. "Depends on her gut. That contrast from the CT scan yesterday? Still sittin' high up in her intestines this mornin'. Nothin's movin'. It's called gastroparesis."

She says the word like it's an heirloom, something quaint to be found at an antique shop. But it's not. It's serious. Deadly.

When the nurse leaves the room, I belly up to the unattended computer cart and read Mama's chart. One diagnosis leaps out: adult failure to thrive.

I Google it: A syndrome of global deterioration in adults with multiple chronic conditions that causes loss of function and health.

Well, shit. She might not make it. She might not make it!

The rooms in our house shake. Doors slam shut. That reality lands in my heart like one of Mama's verbal grenades, threatening to shake loose everything I've been trying so hard to hold together.

I'm undeterred. I leave a kiss on Mama's forehead that's still hot, and head back over the mountain to care for her dogs. Iris is back in Atlanta. The hotel feels far away. But Mama's house still needs tending.

Finally the HVAC team arrives to install that miracle gifted by The Roberts family. Two sweet-faced young men crawl beneath the house like mechanical surgeons, replacing old rusted ductwork, pulling out the decayed unit. I sit in the living room on the couch with the dogs. Suddenly, I hear it—whoosh! Warm air spilling from the vents in Mama's house for the first time in many years.

The house is breathing. TPN for her. Heat for the house. We're feeding everything that matters.

The GoFundMe keeps growing. Iris is matching every donation, dollar for dollar. A West Coast friend's contribution pushes us past five figures! Hot water heater? Getting replaced. Sink? Leaky faucet? On the list.

Still, Ruth is there, always the whisper in the back of my mind:

She might not make it.

She curls tight around my ribs. I realize just how entwined we are, not just me and Ruth, me and Mama. Her body was my first home. She says I curled so close against her spine in the womb, my face bore the imprint when I came out. "You looked like a Klingon," she tells me, deadpan and serious. It was a strange way to start a lifelong relationship with someone who loved me, but didn't really like me. I'm pretty sure the outline of her spine is still etched in my face, if you look hard enough. A birthmark of unrequited closeness.

And even now, through all of it, we still laugh sometimes.

I call her my "Old Woman," just like Dad used to. I threaten to crawl right back inside her V-A-G-I-N-A, spelling it out like a six-year-old with a megaphone. She groans. Rolls her eyes. "Damn kid," she mutters. "You say the weirdest shit."

It's love. Strange. Hard. Real. Ours.

She treats me like I'm fourteen. A fuck-up. Too much. Too loud. Too intense. Too loud and out of control, like her mother was. In her eyes, I'll never grow up.

That's fine. I don't need her to validate who I am. I just need her to know I'm here. That she can lean on me. That she can trust me. I trust myself. That's the difference now. I know I've changed. I've been born and reborn a thousand times since I was first born to her. That's enough. That's all I need to know.

Midweek, I call Big Brother. I'm not asking him to come and help, I just want him to know how serious this is. He's calm. Always is. I'm the hot mess. He's cool like water. Over the years, we've grown into a kind of truce, maybe even friendship. That's pretty radical for siblings that were close when we were young, we had to stay close. As we became teenagers, we found every possible way to tell each other how much we hated each other.

Now I send him funny memes. Out of the blue, he'll text back: "I love you very much, Jen. I am so proud of you. Proud to be your Big Brother. Always have been, always will be."

We survived our childhood in our own ways, and became everything we needed when we were kids: A good dad. A mom who stayed. We're two kids who learned how to mother and father without really being mothered or fathered.

The cold and unforgiving weather returns. And with it, some help we didn't see coming. A land surveyor named Bill Hill shows up. He's a friend of Nina Roberts, a donor to the GoFundMe campaign. He walks the driveway where Mama's been having flooding since a new development was built on the backside of her property. He snaps photos of the lack of drainage. "They can't make their runoff your mom's problem," he says. "Keep your receipts. I'll write a letter to the city."

He limps back to his truck, Ruth and I track bodies in pain instinctively, we know what it looks like when every step is measured. Our radar for pain is strong, you might say we have a keen pain-dar. I offer him water. He waves it off. "Nah, I got a bad back. Had a bunch of surgeries." "Me too," I say. "I've had some surgeries too. Yah, my spine is a real beat-up mess..." He looks at me again, differently now, like suddenly we're a family connected by chronic pain. Then pulls out a square of paper from his wallet, hands it to me like a gift, it reads like a prayer. Testimony. His healing story, a life surrendered to Jesus.

I'm not Christian, but I do love Jesus. I trust and believe in the power of prayer. In love. We never turn away blessings in this house! I accept his paper offering. Gratefully. He doesn't ask to pray, which is common around these parts. He just smiles. "I'm glad I came," he says, a twinkle in his eye. "I'll let ya know what I find out."

Earlier in the week, I asked Nina to reach out to her landscaper about spreading the gravel. She not only gets him, she pays for all the work. So many gifts for our family.

Aurelio arrives Friday. "A-u-r-e-l-i-o," he says slowly. "If you can't say it, call me Sanchez." "I'll call you Aurelio," I smile. I'm sure to pronounce his name perfectly every time.

"I've been here before," he says. "I know your mom." "She's really sick." He nods. "She's a good lady."

He builds a perfect gravel path through the newly

enclosed backyard, one that'll keep Mama safe. Then he says, "I know a guy who is a carpenter, a handyman. Miguel. I'll send him."

Miguel shows up the next day. Soft-eyed. Quiet confidence. He says he taught himself carpentry when his childhood home burned down in Mexico. He opens the back door of his trailer like a magician, revealing a dazzling showcase of tools. Exactly what we need.

I show him around Mama's house. We agree on the scope of work and a fair price.

I tell him, "You know those HGTV shows with big before-and-after reveals? That's what I want. Magic. Big magic." He gets started without hesitation, he prepares to spray the walls of my old, soon-to-be new room with primer, just as something grabs at my gut.

Check the vent, Ruth commands.

I remember the too-big HVAC filter I never returned to the store, leaving the vent wide open without a filter. We leap into action, find it just in time to jam it into the opening before all that wet paint gets into Mama's brand-new HVAC system.

We save the house. Again. Listen, every house needs a watchdog, a cat, a crow on the fence or a lizard at the window. Someone who spots what others miss. Someone who guards not just the door, but the soul.

Ruth — 1996

*S*ome repairs happen in drywall and ductwork. Others happen in places no one sees. Jen is laying hands on both. Every patched hole, repaired vent, gust of warm air in Mama's crumbling house is part of a larger medicine. A slow, strange alchemy that moves backward through time—through grief and jail and mother-wounds and missed appointments. Back through the years when love came laced with chaos, and survival was the only goal.*

Love didn't always look like love back then. Sometimes it looked like running when she should have stayed. Sometimes it looked like staying when she should have run. Sometimes it looked like taping over what you weren't allowed to show.

Even then, something sacred remained. A guard dog. A daughter. An unbreakable commitment. Let me show you where the foundation cracked and our road to healing quietly continued. Let me take you there. Even in the darkest backrooms, I was guarding our perimeter.

Everyone at the club calls her Kit.

"My name's Kit, 'cause I'm made of parts—lots of parts, like a kit," she jokes, grinning wide, her lipstick slightly smeared but still confident. She says it like a punchline, but it holds like a truth.

It's 1996. Jen is twenty-three and spinning on the edge. Up on a high wire with no net, toes poking through fishnet hose, smeared mascara, holding on for dear life.

Nights find her dancing at Larry's Lounge—a low-slung, windowless strip club on the highway in the middle of nowhere. Blaring music. Sticky floors. A spotlight that doesn't care who you are or who you want to be. Clowns love the spotlight. Everyone loves a clown. Kit fits right in.

She wears corsets that barely hold together. High heels mended with duct tape. She gets good at cutting medical tape—titty tape—into perfect little circles to cover her nipples, just enough to satisfy state law. She's seen what happens when girls forget. Vice cops come in all the time. Arrests. Fines. Fingerprints. She's careful. Mostly.

Crown Royal bags double as tip jars, the gold tassels swinging with hip sways. Singles, fives, tens, all of it swept up and stuffed into her bag. The cash piles up. Then disappears again in the inescapable pull of the illegal video slot machines near the bar.

The real money? That's in the back. In the VIP room, where the light disappears, and the rules blur. Pudge is the club's dealer and part-time loan shark. He keeps her supplied. He likes her, says she's got fire. He's always willing to trade for favors.

Jen—Kit—is loud, sharp, impossible to ignore. Her body becomes a broadcast tower beaming at any man for attention. For money. Her laughter is a defense mechanism. Her attention-seeking isn't just a wound. It's a survival skill. Look at me. See me. Pay me. Don't forget me. Don't you know I'm important?

Cocaine comes fast and easy, they call the dressing room *The Crack Den*. Lines snorted off toilet tanks, red lipstick kisses smeared on the mirror. Gnashing teeth. Pupils like floodlights. Up all night. Body aching from the stage, from the chase, from the weight of wanting more but not having any good idea on how to get it.

One bright point of grace breaks through: a court order. Brice is forced to pay child support. The lawyer Mama hired makes it stick and steady money drawn right from his paycheck means bills are paid. Groceries appear. Rent is covered. Days blur into nights. One shift into another. One line into the next. The mask of Kit stays on longer and longer. The lights stay on later and later. She's more of an addict than a mom. Not unlike Dad. Not unlike the man she swore she'd never be like. Sometimes I watched from the back corner of her mind, totally unseen. Just making sure she didn't die. Mama and Lamar step in to take care of Frannie full-time.

It hurts to admit it, but sometimes the truth hurts. During this season, Jen's bad decision to be a stripper, and ultimately an addict, becomes another trauma in Frannie's life. Despite the monkey on her back, Jen shows up in less-than-conventional ways. She's stretched thin, sleep-deprived and strung out, but never misses a therapy appointment. Never skips an IEP meeting. She scribbles the dates in pen. Writes reminders on the back of gum wrappers. She might arrive in cutoff shorts and smeared eyeliner, smelling like a bunch of bad decisions, but she's there. Every time. Eyes sharp. Her voice is always just a little louder than everyone else's. She fights with the fierceness of a mama bear knowing no one else will speak up.

When the school repeatedly locks Frannie in a "time-out closet" under the stairs, a dark, narrow space barely big enough for a folding chair, Jen loses it. Not emotionally. Not irrationally. Legally. Righteously.

"If it's not on her IEP, it's illegal! You can't put her in there. By law."

Her voice rings true like a weather siren. She's done her

research. Read the IEP laws. She is *not* backing down. She's right. They stop. No more closets. No more isolation passed off as discipline. Jen doesn't have it all together, but she's Frannie's sword and shield. Even at their messiest, it's undeniable that they belong to each other.

Jen keeps showing up. And fucking up. The spiral tightens. After a night of partying, she's pulled over. DUI. Arrested. She calls Mama collect from Huntsville City Jail.

"This is the operator. You have a collect call—" Mama answers, "Yah." "Mama? I need help."

Mama bails her out. Picks her up downtown. No lecture. Just looks at her and asks one hard and unflinching question: "You gotta problem?" Jen nods yes and looks out the window. That's enough.

Mama and Lamar move her out of the apartment and into a small rental house across town to detox. Two bedrooms. One bathroom, a leaky faucet, and a rust-stained tub. Cheap rent. No club. No coke. No Pudge. Just Jen. Sweat. And skin-crawling withdrawals. Her body aches with pain. Her thoughts scrambled eggs. The silence in that house is louder than the music ever was at Larry's Lounge.

Mama drops in several times a week. Not gently. Not sweetly. Just efficiently. She pushes open the door like it offends her. Brings groceries, packets of ramen, bananas, milk, ginger ale—then critiques the mess "You need to wash all those dishes. Frannie can't live like this."

She washes piles of laundry with tight-lipped precision. Changes Frannie's sheets, muttering about the smell. Leaves the house cleaner, and colder. No comfort. No eye contact. Just *help*. The kind that feels like an inspection.

Lamar is quieter. He fixes what's broken, the faucet, a bent cabinet hinge, without saying much. His presence hums at the edges. Steady. Unspoken. Maybe the closest thing to peace Jen gets in that house.

Jen stays in bed for days. Then weeks. Then months pass. Sometimes her skin hurts so bad she wants to peel it right off. Her mind blanks out completely. She stares at the ceiling, counting spins of the ceiling fan, trying not to think. I watched her become invisible. I followed her trail. If you've ever left a part of yourself behind, I promise it waited. It might still be waiting.

Frannie's voice filters in from the next room, cartoons, giggles, tiny tantrums. Manageable. Sometimes Jen cries. Sometimes she doesn't feel anything at all. Totally numb. Sometimes she just lies there wanting to disappear into the bed.

Healing isn't soft. It's this: the fight to stay alive, someone banging pots in the kitchen, judging your messy house and your messy life, keeping you fed while you detox off cocaine. Mama didn't offer tenderness, but she kept coming. And that, somehow, is its own kind of love. Even when it stings.

The fog lifts slowly, but surely. Just in time to make another questionable decision. Valentine's Day, 1997. Mama shows up with heart-shaped boxes of candy from the Dollar Store. Frannie eats them while Jen flips through classifieds at the kitchen table, when sees it: A five-bedroom house in a nice part of town. A pool. A deck. Rent's high. Deposit worse.

She calls her old friend Naze from the strip club. "It's got a pool. I'll keep the pool blue. We could split it." "Fabulous," Naze says. "Let's go see it."

To get the deposit, Jen borrows from Pudge. Again.

The house was way too big, but it was theirs, for a while. A makeshift lesbain commune. Naze and her girlfriend Jamie took one side. Jen and Frannie claimed the other. Dogs roamed freely between them, peeing on the carpet, barking at invisible threats. No one cleaned the poop. The pool went murky green fast, algae blooming like green rebellion. Fights sparked over dishes, bills, over who left the gate open again. The big house was loud and unruly and full of life.

Mama hated it. And yet, she came. She'd show up with bags of groceries she probably couldn't afford, drop them on the chipped tile counter with a sigh, and start wiping things down without asking. She moved through the wreckage like a judgmental saint, grumbling, muttering under her breath, but showing up all the same.

"You dyke's live like pigs!," she barked one afternoon, eyeing the pizza boxes, fruit flies, the lace bras hanging from the doorknob.

Jen rolled her eyes and laughed, but part of her was glad. Especially when Lamar came. He didn't judge. He just smiled like it made his day to be there.

When the refrigerator broke, Mama and Lamar hauled a secondhand one over in the back of his truck. It had a dent in the door and smelled bad, but it worked.

They tried to muscle it through the front door, Mama barking instructions, Jen pushing from the back, Lamar guiding the dolly from the stoop. It was a tight squeeze. The fridge caught on the doorframe. Then, with a lurch, the weight shifted and the whole thing tipped over, crashing right onto Lamar.

"Oh, shit!" Jen shrieked, leaping forward to help. "I told you not to angle it that way!" Mama snapped, rushing in with panic hidden behind her irritation.

Lamar just groaned, rolled out from under that metal beast like a turtle flipped over, and sat up, smiling through the pain, "Told ya I was tougher than I look."

Later that week, Mama came back with food, boxed mac and cheese, dented cans of vegetables, frozen mystery meats. She opened the fridge that nearly killed Lamar and started restocking it like it was no big deal.

She didn't say she loved Jen. She didn't have to. She came. She scrubbed counters. She pointed at the bathtub and muttered, "That damn thing needs some bleach."

Judgmental as ever. Helpful in her own weird ways.

Then, the warrant comes. Jen never showed up to court for the DUI. Her driver's license is suspended. She's in serious trouble now.

She comes to Mama and Lamar, hoping to disappear into the walls of their house as she explains: "I owe Pudge money. Plus. There's...there's a warrant."

Mama doesn't blink. "What are ya gonna do about it?"

No softness. Just cold hard truth.

The next day, they call Dad. The one person who knows this flavor of rock bottom by heart. He's three years clean and sober, still living in California.

"I'll come help you," he says. And he does.

In January 1998, he drove cross-country with the help of Big Brother. Dad and his weenie dog move into a small house high up Green Mountain. Jen and Frannie join, bringing two dachshunds.

There's a plan, a family agreement: Jen will face the court. Pay off Pudge. Enroll in community college. Dad will care for Frannie. It's fragile. But real.

In that little house on the mountain, surrounded by dogs, debt, and the faint scent of redemption, a different kind of home begins to take shape. Not built from beams or bricks, but from something older, a willingness to help. This is the beginning of a long, winding path back to herself. I was there for all of it. Watching the doors. Making maps. Waiting for her return. It hurts not to be known. But love waits. Dogs always wait.

Ruth on Loyalty in the Long Silence

I'm bossy, yes.
But don't get it twisted,
I'm not an attack dog.
I'm a guard dog.
A working dog.
I have a job.
And I take it seriously.
Some dogs protect flocks of sheep.
Some stand watch over land, or livestock, or junkyards.
Me?
I protect Jen.
Jen is my flock.
My field.
My home.
My purpose.
My everything.
She knows I'll always be here.
And I will.
Until my service is complete.
Until the energy of my being reweaves itself into
some new, watchful form,
maybe a hummingbird next time,
or the rustle in the trees just before a storm.

Because hypervigilance doesn't die.
It just transforms.
Of course, I'm not a regular dog.
I don't chase squirrels.
I don't knock over the trash,
though I have knocked over a few illusions.
I live in the aether.
Inside of Jen.
I'm what you'd call a part of her,
her vigilance.
An energy of alertness.
A thread of devotion braided into her spine.
I'm the whisper in her body before danger registers.
The twitch in her gut that says, *don't go there.*
The sudden stillness that means something's off.
Have you ever felt that?
I move freely through space and time.
That's the perk of being an inner dog.
I can bring you stories from long ago—
from the years Jen and I weren't in sync.
When we didn't speak.
Oh, I was there.
Every step.
I watched her stumble through wreckage.
Run headfirst into heartbreak with her eyes half-closed
and her heart wide open.
I barked.
I circled.
I tried to intervene.
But we didn't know how to reach each other.
Not yet.
And let me tell you, for me, that was the hardest part.

Not the danger.
Not the chaos.
The silence.
I gnawed at her belly,
rattled her ribcage with anxiety.
Pissed metaphorical warnings all over our perimeter.
Made messes in the name of safety.
But what good is a bark,
if no one is listening?
That's the lonely part of being internal.
People think the threats are all out there.
But inside?
Inside is a carnival of clanging bells,
whack-a-mole memories,
and broken speakers playing the same old mix tapes
on loop.
Inside is where the real noise lives.
Old beliefs.
Inherited guilt.
Shame.
Hardwiring gone sideways.
The echoes of other people's fears.
Other people's stories and voices.
Her mind used to be too loud for anything steady,
let alone me.
There was no space for creativity.
No room for quiet.
No opening for loyalty.
And still, I waited.
That's what good dogs do.
Even when she ignored me,
I circled her heart like a sentinel.

Never judged.
Never left.
Even when she walked right toward fire,
all I wanted was for her to turn back.
But her path is hers.
Not mine to control.
My job isn't to steer the journey.
My job is to stand guard.
Even now, I feel the old pull to bark too loud.
Snap too fast.
Old instincts don't vanish.
They just soften.
But here's the difference now—
Jen hears me.
We talk.
We share space.
Sometimes we laugh about how uptight we are.
She doesn't always listen right away,
but she does turn toward me, eventually.
That's the miracle.
That's our redemption.
Because here's the truth,
and I hope you tattoo this somewhere deep inside
your heart:
It's hard to protect what hasn't been claimed.
Hard to guard a house no one's come home to.
You've got to return to yourself,
open that inner door,
before your dog—or cat, or rat, or winged beetle
guardian, can do their job.
Otherwise, we're just lost parts of you pacing the halls.
Roaming room to room.

Unheard.
Unloved.
Unseen.
But once you open that door—
even just a crack?
We're right here.
Ready.
Loyal.
Here for you.
Always.

—Ruth

Chapter 6:

Distilling

Jen — Winter 2022

Miguel rolls another coat of glossy white paint across the baseboards. The untouched room, the one with the rat and the maggots, the one avoided like plague, is transforming into something else entirely. He'll lay fresh subflooring over the cracked linoleum, then top it with oversized, self-adhering tiles. Patchwork meets potential. It won't be perfect, but it doesn't have to be.

Honestly? It looks pretty damn good. He's also agreed to repair the rotten framing under the laundry room where the water heater leaked into the crawlspace. He'll patch holes with those same sticky tiles. They won't match, but they'll hold.

Just like we do.

With so much repaired and more underway, I turn to the next beast: the electrical panel. The local guy I texted last week ghosted me, can't say I blame him. That rusted panel looks like it'll electrocute anyone in close proximity. I found another company online, based in Huntsville. Veteran-owned. That feels right, Mama's a veteran, after all.

A woman answers. I tell her everything: Mama's illness, Lamar's death, the GoFundMe. She listens, *really* listens. Then says: "You know there's a community of Marines around here who might help your mom?"

I blink. "Seriously?"

"Yep. I'll talk to my husband. He'll come out next week and take a look."

Mama's still curled up in that dim hospital room, more asleep than awake. Nausea clings to her like a second skin now, sour, tight, inescapable. Her gut still won't wake up. That TPN is keeping her stable, a slow drip through the port in her arm, bypassing digestion altogether—liquid survival. But there aren't any answers. No plans. Just this limbo between pain and prognosis. When she comes home, she'll need nursing care.

Maybe forever.

I don't know how I'll manage, my family needs me in Atlanta. Frannie needs routine. Iris needs a partner. Our house needs me back. But this is where I am. This is what's happening.

At the hotel, another conference rolls in—this time it's judges, bailiffs, and clerks. The parking lot fills up with cruisers gleaming under the streetlights. Badges. Boots. Baritone voices.

Twenty-five years ago, I would've bolted right outta this place. Scanned for exits and halfway gone before anyone even saw me. My body knows all about running away. But now? I stay. I breathe. I show up. It's not that I'm fearless— it's that I'm here. I'm staying.

Frannie's over it. The novelty of our hotel life has worn too thin. Cabin fever's got her climbing the walls. She starts leaving the room when I'm out—first for snacks, then towels at the front desk, then just roaming the halls. She's lonely. Stir-crazy. Her spark is dimming under the weight of so many days alone. Even unlimited movies and junk food have lost their magic.

Routine is everything for her. In Atlanta, she'll have it again. Even though Iris works during the day, she'll be home at night. There'll be rhythms again. Familiar sounds. Predictable light. We decide: it's time. Frannie and the pups will go back.

It twists my heart, but I trust the universe. Trust Ruth. Trust the system of vigilance we've built with all our tabs open. I'll be in one home here. One home there. All of it is real. All of it interconnected.

They'll be okay. We'll make sure of it.

Iris and I pack the room. Frannie fills her backpack with games, chargers, treasures—every little thing that's helped us through. We don't forget Wion, Wicky's ragged lion soul-mate. Bags multiply. I wonder, how does that always happen? I laugh, shaking my head. "How did we collect all this shit?"

Iris snorts. Frannie giggles. We laugh together, tired, real laughter. Then it hits me. This room, a small cranberry and beige space—it held us so perfectly. When everything else fell apart, this was our soft place to land. Our bunker. Our nest. I'll never forget it.

We share a three-way hug, messy, full of love. Frannie nuzzles in tight.

Iris kisses my forehead, "Take it easy, babe," she says. "Your body can't take much more."

She's not wrong. Everything hurts. Everything in me is trying to stay strong while begging for rest.

They leave me with only my things. Just the clutter of one person now. The echo of our family laughter still warm in the corners of the room. A piece of me goes with them. A piece of them stays. We head down into the underground parking garage together. Iris loads the car, I hold the dogs' leashes while Frannie buckles up and settles in. "You be a good girl, okay?" "I will, Mama, I promise."

I close the car door. The engine starts. I watch them as they pull away, and stand there for a long minute after they're gone. Quiet. Still. Letting the silence settle over me. Alone without my pack. I listen for the birds in the ceiling— nothing. Not even a chirp. Even the parking garage is quiet. The whole building sighs with me. Like it knows our page has turned.

I'm not checking out of the hotel yet. We're keeping the room through the week, just in case. Mama might get worse. Or better. Plus my new room, my Fantasy Island beach retreat, still isn't ready, a bed-frame, mattress, and new sheets are on the way. So tonight, I'll sleep in Mama's bed with her dogs.

The weather's gone completely sideways. More snow. More ice. At least we have heat, thanks to the generosity of the Roberts family. I pass time organizing Mama's office, cleaning and arranging her vintage salt and pepper shakers.

That old fridge is gone now, hauled off by junk guys, the whole house feels lighter.

I unbox and set up the electric toothbrush I bought her. She's gonna love it. I take those breaks like I promised Iris, my body relieved by some rest. The dogs approve. I scroll online. Text Frannie hourly, I need to stay close. I continue researching Mama's conditions. Hypervigilance with Wi-Fi access? Straight-up spellcraft. It's how Ruth and I self-soothe.

Miguel works late into the evening. Painting walls. Laying tiles. Transforming rooms while I rest my body and hold a larger vision.

Each day he arrives quiet, focused. Music low. Tools precise. He doesn't talk much, just gets to work, like he can sense something scared beneath this mess.

The next night, he pops his head into the hallway before heading out.

"Ms. Jen? I'm leaving now. You can check the room—but be careful, the paint is still wet."

"Thank you, Miguel! Drive safe!"

He nods, smiles, then disappears. I wait until his truck crunches down Mama's gravel driveway, tail lights fading into dusk down the highway.

Ready to go to the beach?

We always wanted to go to Fantasy Island. Let's savor this!

Ruth's voice hums low in my chest.

We've earned it.

I step inside, and cannot believe my eyes. The room is unrecognizable.

A real life glow-up. Blueish-green walls that shine like sea glass. Glossy white trim like a satin ribbon wrapped around a Tiffany box. Creamy colored tiles underfoot, soft light bouncing from every surface. The difference is night and day, like life-force returned to a body after a near-death experience.

I stand there, still, letting the moment fully hit me. Then tears come, sudden and real. This room, it mirrors my own becoming. I used to think I had to fix everything inside me. All the cracks, all the noise, all my bad decisions. Now I know I don't have to fix it. I just have to stay with myself. Stay with the mess of being me. Stay with the pain. Stay long enough to see what wants to grow out of the shadows, out of the dark. It's weird the way the cracks became the map.

I'm proud of you. Proud of us. Look what we did.

We did it together—me, you, Miguel, Iris, Frannie, the dogs, the universe, and a whole lot of Ruth.

This. This is what I mean by alchemy: transformation born of attention. Magic wrapped in wreckage. Grace braided with good old-fashioned grit. This is what it looks like when me and the universe are all lined up.

We transformed the worst room in the house into a sacred space, just like I've been doing inside myself, all along. Not all at once. Not with any certainty, just a soul hunch that underneath all that brokenness in me, something was waiting to be found: wholeness.

I didn't find that wholeness by fixing my broken parts. I found it by staying in the dark long enough to learn to see. To reclaim my wholeness. Death came for me as a baby. She left me a message: I have a gift for you—but you'll only find it in the dark. That's where you'll earn your night vision. That's where freedom lives.

It turned out, Death was right. I stopped running. Stopped contorting myself into shapes and stories that didn't fit, I started asking better questions:

What if I'm not broken, just many parts? Who am I when no one's watching? Who am I when I'm not trying to be something else?

I didn't wanna end up like my dad. He was brilliant, but splintered, unreachable, and wholly irresponsible. At many points in my life, I was too. I made a lot of his mistakes. He had a beautiful mind, but no awareness of it. I wanted to know my mind. I felt sure one way to avoid what felt like my fate of like-father-like-daughter was to do something different. Try something different. Be something different.

I found that awareness in nature. In myself. In stillness. In the willingness to feel what it is to be me. To look inside myself and see what I never wanted to see. Feel what I avoided feeling. Walk straight up to what I was always afraid of inside myself, and look it straight in the eye. Face-to-face. It hasn't been easy making peace with everything that's happened, in my life, and the life that has lived through me.

I lied. I stole. I let Frannie down. Many times. Sure there were reasons, but the fact is I made a lot of shitty decisions and repeated the very same patterns that hurt me as a child. I still think about that gold ring I stole from Mama when I was a teenager. Like maybe if I scrub hard enough at the memory, it'll flake off and disappear. But I can't erase my past. I don't want to anyway. Those bad decisions shaped me as much as the good. I was just trying to be loved. Trying to make my own way, so often the wrong way. I was always trying to matter to someone.

I thought I had to be someone else to be worthy. Someone different. Definitely not me. But the truth? I just needed to come home. I wasn't bad. I wasn't stuck, destined to turn out like Dad, no matter how many times Mama said I was. I've always been a transformative being. Never just one thing. I'm many things. Messy, complicated, full of false starts, timing issues, and weird harmonies, but I'm still a soul full of music. My own kind of music. Not some fixed identity. More like trees. Bent in places. Scarred in others. Always reaching for the light. That's what I've been doing all my life, twisting toward the sun, towards something true in me I couldn't quite name yet, but knew it was in here.

The next day, I woke up a sad pancake. That's chronic illness code for too many overnight flips, not enough sleep. My body feels like it's been steamrolled in dreams I can't remember. My spine is furious. Hips spitting fire. Everything in me is having a full-blown meltdown. The Chronic Pains were up all night jamming, our whole house was loud.

I swallow three Tylenol as a truce offering. Maybe they'll go to bed. I doubt it. Then drop tincture under my tongue. Stretch my arms out wide. OUCH! Don't stretch! I try to rally my tired, tattered body that just wants to be left alone. Every joint groans like a door forced open too many times.

We've got shit to do. I shuffle to the sink. Wash my face.

Just start with this.

Miguel's coming. So's the electrician. I'm nervous. That electrical panel could eat up our whole budget. I've held off buying the sink and faucet until I know more.

Around noon, a monster truck pulls in. Flared fenders. Tinted windows. Big gravel-crunching energy. A man sits inside, talking on the phone. He doesn't get out right away.

Ruth's ears twitch: *If he's a creeper, we can take him.*

Miguel's here.

Emergency Preparedness Plan: Engaged.

He steps down, smiling. Sunglasses still on. He says something, I can't make it out.

I wave, point to my ears, "Traffic!" He waves back and moves closer, "Hi there! I'm Mike. For the electrical estimate?"

We talk. I tell him about Mama. Her time in the Marines. She and her twin brother enlisted the minute they turned eighteen. I tell him about how sick she is. He listens.

Inside, he walks through the house like a tuning fork. "No GFCIs. No smoke detectors. That outlet? Burned out. Don't plug anything into it, it could start a fire."

My stomach drops. Mama was *that* close to dying just trying to stay warm. Just trying to stay alive. Back outside, he asks, "Estimate by email?" "Yes, please." "We'll talk soon."

I collapse onto Mama's bed. My body's wrecked. I try to nap. Ruth stays awake. We're wracked with worry about how we're gonna pay for a whole bunch of work.

I wake to a text from Mike: **Sent the estimate. Let me know.**

I open the PDF, fully bracing for the worst.

Thousands of dollars' worth of work—new panel, all new outlets, detectors.

Total cost? Five dollars.

He got the materials donated. A volunteer crew of Marines—The Semper Fi Task Force—will do the whole installation. All I have to pay for is the permit.

My text back to him: **Is this real?**

His text: **Just tell your mom to get better. We'll take care of her house.**

That night, I lay there in Mama's bed, dogs curled all around me, my voice hoarse from telling the story to anyone who'd listen. A five-dollar miracle smack dab in the Alabama mud. How could I not believe in magic when blessings like this unfold? I've always trusted synchronicity. This confirms that the universe is in our corner.

Ruth — 1998

You'd think a house couldn't hold so much. But some houses—like some hearts—get stretched far way beyond their square footage. Some houses and hearts break open under that weight, but somehow, still become vessels for light.

Jen's cleaning one room at a time. Laying fresh tile over Mama's old heartbreak. Painting past mold, the rat, the maggots. Scrubbing walls like she's wringing out forgotten family ghosts. Every corner isn't just repair—it's a retrieval. Of worth. Of place. Of selves. For both her and Mama.

When Jen finally sits down in that ocean-colored room, takes in the full blown miracle of clean walls, of light that doesn't leave? That's not just rest. It's a revolution. To really explain the transformation, I need you to come back with me. Back to where the promise of safety met the heartbreak of collapse.

Because the story of this house doesn't begin with a fresh coat of paint. It begins again in the paradox of what is falling apart and what is coming together.

Big Brother drives Dad cross-country from California in a busted, sputtering van. No one talks about what happened on that drive. But something in the air arrives with them, heavy, unspeakable, and sharp around the edges.

Big Brother is thirty. Still stoic. Just out of the military. His silence has become a shield. His eyes are hard. His body's tight like it's trying to protect itself from something no one saw. When they pull into Mama's gravel driveway, the air is thick with tension. Jen doesn't know the full story. There's history in that van. Shit went down. Mama snaps a picture of the three of them to remember the moment.

Big Brother made the drive. He brought the man who broke him over and over since he was a boy across the country because his little sister needed help. He always showed up for her like that, a kind of bravery the world doesn't reward. But I saw it. I always did.

At one point, Dad, true to form, floated the idea that she could run. Flee. Disappear, like he always had. But Big Brother and Lamar squashed it before it could take root. She wasn't going to vanish. She had to face things. Get right with the law. And everybody knew it.

Jen can't worry about what happened on the drive, Dad's here! He's really here. They're together again, father and daughter, after all this time. It's everything she ever wanted since Mama moved everyone to Texas. It's a do-over.

They move into a small rented house perched atop Green Mountain, with a living room overlooking Huntsville. They call their beat-up car Cecil the Vessel. The plan is clear:

Dad's staying home to care for Frannie. He'll handle the house and the dogs. Manage the bills. Jen will go to school and get off probation. It's the first structure she and Frannie have had in years. Maybe ever.

A colossal steel desk swallows her whole. The probation office smells like dirty carpet and burnt coffee. Fluorescent lights flicker overhead, sharp as the judgment in the room. It feels more like another point of punishment than a place for second chances.

Jen's twenty-five. This is her final mandated check-in after the DUI, detox, the missed court date, the whole unraveling. Seven days in jail. Six months supervised probation. Six more unsupervised. A weekly risk-reduction class. Nineteen hundred dollars in fines. She's carried the weight of every step towards this fresh start. Now, all that's left is this moment.

The lanky officer behind the desk flips through her file like he's hunting down a weakness. Her last name —Peer— echoes across the pages like an invitation to look deeper.

"Well... Jennifer." He clears his throat slowly, he wants her to know he's in control. "Last meeting." He glances quickly at her over thick black glasses. "You've done what the judge asked. Paid your fines. I see you're goin' to school?"

"Yes, sir. Community college. Second semester—I'm taking summer classes. Hoping to transfer to Athens State."

She straightens her crooked spine. Lifts a smile like a tattered flag she's pieced together herself, oh so carefully, slowly, one good decision at a time after a long string of bad ones.

The chair beneath her creaks like the floor is going to drop out. She's ready for the fall.

"Uh huh. Good for you." He raises one unimpressed eyebrow. A pause long enough to wilt her courage.

"So long as you stay out of trouble for the next six months...this whole thing? *Poof.* Expunged. Understand?"

"Yes, sir, I do," she says, her words steady, palms damp.

She understands what it means to sit across from someone who sees your past like a checklist of failures, but can't seem to recognize your future. Who doesn't see you. She knows the cost of getting clean, the way hope feels heavy, stitched together from scraps. She understands what it is to cling to a second chance like a fragile object through a room full of tripwires, hoping you don't drop it before you reach the door.

That same summer, Lamar handles the next part of the family agreement. He walks into Larry's Lounge to pay off Jen's debt to Pudge, the loan shark. He hands over the borrowed deposit, plus three hundred extra, just to make sure it's really done.

She learns later: both men were armed. Lamar—our blue-eyed angel of calm—walked straight into the underworld without flinching, ready to do whatever it took. He never made her earn his love. That was Lamar. Always showing up. Always filling in where Dad couldn't. His belief in her was total. A kind of inner scaffolding, something solid to cling onto, holding up parts of our foundation no one else could see were broken.

Now, with Dad beside her too, Jen sees the best in herself. He's not the drunk Mama warned her about. He's not broken. He's brilliant. Charismatic. Spiritually voracious. A soul-miner who speaks in riddles, quoting metaphysics, Jung, and supermarket tabloids with equal gravitas. He makes her believe she could be more than a screw-up. That she's wise, creative, and smart.

They belt out Andrea Bocelli's *Con te Partirò*, piping from a red boombox like it's sacred music. Like they're monks in a monastery made of linoleum and old love.

With you, I shall leave. The words aren't translated, but they're felt. Something about letting go and staying close. About carrying each other into whatever comes next.

They laugh over Dad's famous Glop—a savory mystery stew with ground beef and whatever's in the pantry. They live together. Eat together. Heal, together.

Dad and Frannie click right away. He never flinches when she rages. His work as a psych tech at Agnews State Hospital all those years ago prepared him for this. He knows the drill. He locks up the knives. Sorts the meds. He holds Frannie in a way that makes her feel safe, and teaches Jen to do the same, the subtle mechanics of meltdown management.

Together, she and Frannie move through brutal, ballet-like holds, Frannie's biting teeth turn into tiny weapons. Restraint and ritual. Safety and sweetness. Sweat and piss. Tears and puke, all mingled in their own strange intimacy of survival. A grotesque kind of rebirth. But rebirth, still. Something opens. A bond is forged inside a child that has never bonded. Eye contact happens in moments where there had been none.

In community college, Jen affirms what Dad says, she's smart. *Really* smart. Imagine coming this far in life and being so swept up in the chaos of trauma, that you never have time to realize your potential. Psychology. Writing. Sociology. They light her up. She starts making friends. Becomes a star student.

Her favorite English professor, Dr. Beth Thames hands back a paper—A+. "You're an excellent writer, Jen." "Really?" she asks, eyes wide, voice cracking. "Yes. You have a gift."

Her words land smooth like a goose gliding to still water. Jen writes everything after that with newfound conviction.

Professor Thames helps her get a part-time job tutoring. She starts to believe in herself.

The underworld begins to feel like a memory. She meets Layla at school—bright, witty, book-hungry. They study. Dream. Smoke weed together. Listen to Tori Amos. Take up space in a life that finally feels good for Jen.

More good news: Athens State University accepts her. She never misses school. She earns straight As, except for math, which makes her break out in hives. She pushes through. She's on her way.

Until she isn't. Yellow lights are flickering on the horizon.

Jen's spine, twisted by the late-effects of all that radiation when she was a baby, starts collapsing. Not all at once. Slow in a way that echoes, that makes it hard to breathe. Quiet at first, a faint whisper, until every breath she takes sounds like a dusty organ. She doesn't talk about it much. Braces against chairs. Holds books in the crook of one arm, lifting them both feels like betrayal. Breathing grows harder. A tightness settles in her chest. Pain sharpens. Not just in her back, but in the knowledge that this is the body she has to live in forever.

Mama says, "You're a tough kid. You can handle it. You'll figure it out"

That's the script, isn't it? The capacity for endurance passed off as strength. So she does. She tightens her jaw. Breathes through the pain. Keeps going. Keeps up with school. Keeps moving forward in a body that keeps on keeping on. Because if she stops now, what happens to the family plan? To Frannie? To the life she's built from scraps?

No matter how hard she tries, cracks keep appearing. Dad begins to drift. It starts slowly: a missed bill here, forgotten pickups there, silences that grow longer.

Frannie's back at Mama and Lamar's house more and

more. Jen convinces herself it's just temporary, she's busy with school. Dad needs time to adjust. They'll figure it out.

The cracks widen. Utilities are being shut off. Groceries rot in the fridge. Prescriptions stack up unopened on the counter like silent accusations.

The TV in his room never shuts off. Voices fill the house when no one else is speaking. Dad's door stays closed all the time. Jen swears she hears him talking back to it—not on the phone. Not to himself. To *them*. To the flickering, faceless voices in the box.

Sometimes she knocks. "Dad?" A pause. The TV volume goes up. No answer.

Before the silence, there were good times. Times worth holding on to for dear life. Like when Jen was taking a literature class at the community college. She had to present a visual project, something interpretive. She asked Dad for help. He said yes. She drew the visuals on overhead projector sheets. He rehearsed his narrated part like it was Broadway.

The day of, he stood in front of the whole class in his pressed shirt and delivered the entire piece in his deep, resonant baritone voice, while she changed the slides. They moved as one. She felt proud to have Dad there. She made an A, he was totally invested.

Until he wasn't. One afternoon, while he's out, she follows her sixth sense, that quiet, Ruth-shaped whisper that's never stopped circling our perimeter. Jen stands there for a good long time at the door of his room. Takes a breath. Picks the lock, a trick he himself had taught her.

That smell hits first. Rank. Wrong.

Not just the smell of rot and garbage. It's the smell of betrayal. A trash bag full of beer cans. There's a Rubbermaid tote filled with shit. Not figuratively, literal human shit.

Dad's shit. Betting slips. Notecards scribbled with debts and strange, disjointed thoughts. The scattered evidence of his life unraveling behind the closed door. The worst part? She's not even shocked.

"Jesus Christ. Fuck. Fuck. *FUCK.*"

Her body folds onto his bed, not because of grief, but from the weight of his failures that finally eclipsed any need to stay close to him. Same old Chinese Finger Trap. But this time, she doesn't pull him closer. She pushes inward, and lets him go.

What about the family agreement? What about their plan, that was supposed to hold it all together? She believed in Dad. Big mistake. She stares up at the ceiling, emptied like a junk drawer flipped over. Then reaches for the phone.

"Lamar? Can I come over and talk to you and Mama?" "Sure thing, darlin'. You OK? You and Frannie come for dinner at six. I'm broilin' chicken breasts. Bring your dad a plate home."

"Yah. We're... fine. See you soon."

Christmas, 2000. Just when our house seemed like it might finally stand...everything falls apart. All over again.

Ruth On Our First House

. . . .

You want to talk about loyalty?

Let's talk about her.

Mama.

The one I watched long before Jen ever knew I existed.

She was the first house we lived in.

Our first weather.

Our first frequency.
Our first silence.
Our first sharp edge was also a home.
She wasn't built for tenderness, not the kind Jen needed.
But she also didn't leave.
She showed up in the ways she could.
With food. With folded laundry. With fury.
Some people water you with praise.
Mama watered with presence.
Sometimes just barely.
But it was something.
And I need you to know,
she had her own guard dog, once.
A dog a lot like me.
You don't survive what she did without one.
 I don't know what happened to it.
 Only that somewhere along the way, it went quiet.
Maybe it got locked out.
Maybe it just grew tired of barking where no one listened.
I only know she stopped listening to the voice inside—
the one that tried, more than anything, to protect her
from her terrible things.
She tuned it out so hard,
she couldn't hear much of anything, not even
her own kids.
I remember the way she carried her past,
like heavy furniture she couldn't set down.
Always rearranging.
Always hoping that this time, it might feel like home.
She was scared.
So she got loud.
She was lonely.

So she got mean.
But don't confuse meanness for a lack of love.
That woman loved her kids with a wildness
beyond language.
She showed it in her own dialect:
A waterbed mattress thrown over a fence.
A single squeeze on the shoulder instead of a hug.
I'll say this now,
as someone who's spent a lifetime barking into silence:
Mama didn't fail.
She fragmented.
And fragmentation isn't the same as abandonment.
It's just what happens when you carry more weight than
you were built for,
with no one to help unpack it.
Jen wanted a mother.
She got a survivor.
And survivors don't always get the chance to be soft.
They're still sacred.
Still vital.
Still worthy of respect, even redemption.
So here I am,
Ruth—Mama's daughter's loyal dog-self—
saying the thing that needs to be said:
We don't have to romanticize her to love her.
We don't have to hate her to be honest.
We just have to tell the truth.
That she did her best to live with a broken map,
and somehow still helped carve a path that Jen could walk.
That counts.
That counts for a lot.

—*Ruth*

Chapter 7:

Hallowing

Jen — Winter 2022

The doctor calls with a tone that's both hurried and matter-of-fact. "She doesn't need to be here just to receive nutrition. The risk of contracting COVID remains high if she stays in the hospital."

I get it. They need the beds. I really do understand, but she's not ready to be discharged. A feeding tube isn't a *send-ya-home* kinda thing.

When the charge nurse calls to confirm her release, I push back. "I don't know how to work that tube. You can't send her home until someone shows me what to do."

I press just firmly enough. It works. Mama gets to stay through the weekend. A few more days might make all the difference. They're calling for heavy snow anyway—nobody in Alabama drives in that. Snowfall is one of the rare times that the busy highway in front of Mama's house goes quiet.

Miguel finishes the last of the work. Holes patched. Framing repaired. Tile gleaming. Paint dry. My beach retreat? Officially complete.

Welcome to Fantasy Island—Alabama edition. Me, my island of dreams, and that stubborn broken window that still won't open. Somehow? Everything works. At least in this room.

It's still Mama's old house, same low ceilings, same lingering smell of too many things left unattended for too long. But the energy is different now. The ground feels more stable.

It's okay. Not all rooms need tending right away.

Miguel packs up his immaculate trailer of tools, wiping each one down like a ritual, I head outside to catch him before he leaves, "Hey," I call, my voice hitching a little. "I couldn't have done this without you. I'll never forget what you did for my mom. Thank you."

He turns to me, that boyish grin already spreading. Modest to the bone. He's a good man. Steady hands. Quiet heart. Soul of gold.

"Happy to do it," he says. "You take care of her now, Ms. Jen."

"I will." I look him in the eye. "I hope your life is filled with blessings, my friend."

He nods. "You too." Off he goes, trailer humming behind, taillights winking down the gravel driveway, then down the highway. And something shifts. A loosening in my chest. A doorway to the future cracking open just a teeny tiny crack. We're not done. Not even close. But we're here, living, breathing, and rebuilding right here in *Fantasy Island, Alabama.* Where the palm trees are memories, the sand is mostly dust, and the magic comes one patchwork piece of floor at a time.

There's one big-hearted conundrum left: Lily. She's a sweet goof of a dog—big, joyful, and completely unaware of her size. One wrong jump could dislodge Mama's feeding tube. I can't take the risk.

I called a rescue friend in Atlanta. By some small miracle, she knows a family looking to adopt a third dog. They have two older basset hounds and a big fenced yard.

You gotta jump when the door opens!

So we do.

I arranged to meet Iris halfway between Mama's house and Atlanta early Saturday morning. She'll take Lily the rest of the way.

Meanwhile, I'll be sleeping in my new room for the first time, just a mattress on the floor, but a far cry from that old couch or Mama's bed.

Saturday comes. The handoff goes smoothly. Iris hugs me so tight it feels like home.

"You don't need to worry," she says, gripping Lily's leash. "She's a great dog. Who wouldn't want to love her?"

"I love you, honey."

Just like that, they're off towards Lily's potential new life.

By 11 AM, she calls again. "I'm here. Pulling down their street now—wow, this place is huge. At least five acres fenced. Fingers crossed."

"Okay, babe. Be careful. Keep Lily's leash tight till she's comfortable with the other dogs."

She laughs. "I know, I know. Talk soon."

She puts up with our hypervigilant antics. Some would call it nagging. We call it managing things.

That's right.

An hour and a half later: it's a no-go. The basset hounds growled the whole time. Lily's coming back. I'm disappointed, but mostly for Lily and Iris, who drove hours on hope and a hunch.

"Okay. We'll talk when you get home. We'll try again tomorrow."

We agreed to meet again. Same spot. 8 AM. Round two for the Lily hand-off and a quick hug. I miss Iris more than I let myself feel most days.

The next morning, I stretch across the floor mattress in my retreat, sunlight spills through the window that still won't open. My body always hurts, today is no different, but the sun lifts the pain slightly. Even broken windows let in the light.

Sometimes, especially those.

I used to lay on the couch as a kid and disappear into TV shows for hours, days at time. Shows where people were chosen. Where they belonged. Where wishes came true.

I didn't know it was practice. I thought I was escaping. Maybe I was blueprinting. I never got to Fantasy Island. So I built my own. Here I am. Breathing salt air. Stretching in the sunlight. Waving to Mr. Rourke and Tattoo, they wave back to me. The portal from then to now is real, I walked right through it.

I call Iris. "Hi, babydoll!" Her voice is bright as always.

I hear something in the background. An engine. "Wait—where are you?"

"I decided to surprise you," she says, like it's no big deal. "I'm bringing Lily to your mom's. Just grabbed coffee. Are you good with a soy latte?"

Tears. This woman!

"Oh my Sticky. You didn't have to... Yes. That's perfect. I love you." "Love you too."

Of course she did this. This is who she is. She leads with her whole heart.

She's an excellent pack leader.

It's just the way she's made. Her mom and dad had everything to do with that. Salt of the Earth kind of folks.

When she pulls in, we laugh before we even speak, our smiles say everything. We're grateful. Down-to-the-bone grateful to see each other. To be together.

"I came to set up your bed," she says, smiling. "No more mattress on the floor for you!"

Together, we build the frame. Slide in slats. Attach a soft headboard that's easy on my back. I flop myself down dramatically when it's done, my spine sighing in relief like it dropped a burden it's been carrying since 1998.

"This is heaven," I tell her. "I needed this."

We snap a selfie to remember it—two tired, big-hearted, dog loving queers in the middle of nowhere Alabama, feeling safe together in a house that forgot how to feel safe.

Then she's gone again, back to Frannie, back to the pups, back to the buzz and whirl of Atlanta.

She always shows up. In a million big and little ways.

Later that day, I'm enjoying some rest on the new bed Iris just helped me build. The frame still feels warm from her hands. The mattress finally has a structure. I wanna stay there. Just a few more minutes of rest, then the home infusion provider calls. The voice on the other end is all business. Mama's TPN isn't covered by Medicare. Not unless they cut her open and place a cheaper, more permanent line. If they slice into her body again, sure, then they'll help. But this? This gentler, less invasive, less traumatic way of feeding her? Nope. Not gonna happen. Not unless we pay.

Tell me how that makes sense! She's just barely waking up. Held down a spoonful of fruit. Now we're weighing the risks of surgery against paperwork. I give them my credit card. The lady taking my information is flat. Automatic.

We'll figure it out. We always do.

I wish we didn't have to. I wish staying alive didn't cost an arm and a leg. But I don't have time for contemplating the brokenness of insurance, I have work to do.

Later that evening when I returned to the hospital, I nearly fell over when I walked through the door.

Mama's sitting up in the bed. Not just awake, *upright.* Spine lifted. Eyes alert.

She's holding a styrofoam cup of ice water in two hands, sipping through the bendy straw like a toddler learning how to drink, one cautious slurp at a time.

I stop right there in my tracks. "Mama... you're holding that down?"

Her voice is ragged, gravelly at the edges, but sure,

there's some life there.

"Yep. First thing that hasn't made me sick."

She puts the cup down and picks up a plastic hospital spoon and wobbles it toward her mouth, primitive, clumsy, necessary food. Puréed fruit, peach maybe.

I stand there taking in the scene. The lights are on. The TV's on. Even the sound is on, cooking shows, maybe. Something familiar.

Seems she's back in the world?

The energy in the room has changed. It used to feel like this was a suffocating waiting room for death. Now it feels like someone cracked open a window and let some life in.

The doctor walks in shortly after, chart in hand, eyes crinkle above his mask.

"Can you believe it?"

"No," I say, shaking my head. "I really can't."

"She kept down a nutrition drink last night. Her gut's waking up."

Her gut's waking up!

That vital part of her that digests, absorbs, nourishes. That part was frozen in time. That part that kept trying to leave, decided to stay.

They pull the TPN line. She's coming home. No feeding tube. No machines. Just her. Alive. Sitting up. Spoon in hand. Food going in.

I head over to the store to grab soft things Mama might be able to eat. I pull my aching body towards the baby food aisle, cart squeaking, one wheel getting stuck every few steps so I have to back it up and reset the cart over and over.

My brain's buzzing. My mind won't quit. Ruth, as always, is clocking everything: labels, textures, noises, smells. She always does.

Gotta hurry up and get back to Mama.

In the aisle for baby related things, the shelves are lined with packets of pastel promises for good health and nutrition. Tiny meals for tiny people. Mama's not tiny, but she is fragile. I'm not shopping for a baby, not in the usual sense anyway.

I scan the labels with one eye on the clock, trying to pin down what Mama used to like, sweet, smooth, not too tart. I remember those glass jars of baby food used to come in. Bananas. Sweet potatoes. Peas.

Now they come in handy little pouches. Some are fruity. Some have oats. Some blended so smooth they could be anything. She'll never care what's in them, if it tastes good.

I throw every pouch that might pass her test into the cart, a rainbow of soft offerings in soft packaging. Fuel for her gut learning to work again. Somewhere between an applesauce and prune blend, it hits me: Life feeds itself.

Everything's a cycle.

Mama's baby feeding Mama baby food.

Mama's discharged from the hospital, but there's a hitch. The electrical work the Marines donated will take 48 hours to complete. We need to vacate the house. I decide to board the big dogs at the vet, then bring Mama and the little dogs to our hotel room — the one that transforms once again to hold our family, the same, but differently.

Mama sacks out on the bed where Frannie used to sleep. Watches cooking shows. Sips from baby food pouches. She sleeps a lot. When she's awake, she's quiet, but alert. She's coming back.

I ask, "Mama, I don't want to leave you alone yet. Wanna come to Atlanta for a few days? Frannie's turning thirty-five this weekend. Can you believe it?"

She lights up. "That'd be fun. I'd love that."

She's never seen our new house. I can hardly believe I might get this chance to bring her there. We made a plan to board the big dogs and take the little dogs with us.

While she rests at the hotel, I return to the house to oversee the installation of the latest upgrades.

A new sparkly sink with a sprayer faucet. A bathroom tap that doesn't leak. A grow light for her plant nook. A motion light so she won't trip in the dark.

Some creatures see better in the dark.

But we all do better with a little light!

On the drive to Atlanta Mama reminisces about Lamar. Her voice doesn't shift much, still that same sharp-edged tone, the kind that comes from being a Marine, a mother, and a lifelong survivor all at once. There's something steely in it, even when she's talking about love. It's a weird paradox: a hard, no-nonsense woman recalling the man who made her feel safe.

He made us all feel safe.

"The roads don't look like they used to," she says. "Fewer

billboards back then. Less people. Less noise."

She tells me how Lamar drove her to these same winding roads after they got married. He liked taking her the long way. They used to hold hands between towns, her fingers resting in his hand, it was everything to her. To them.

"He was good to me," she says. Quiet. Flat. Final. Matter of fact. Then we drive in miles of silence.

When we arrive in Atlanta, Frannie's waiting at the end of the driveway, thrilled to see Grandma and the dogs. Pax goes berserk making circles at my feet. Wicky, our blind dog, barks himself hoarse, I kiss every inch of his perfect slick black weenie body. He wiggles and giggles with sheer delight. Mama's little dogs sniff out their new terrain, tails wagging. The whole house hums with our joyous reunion. I lay down in my bed, returning to where this whole journey started. I try to take in the gravity of what's happened.

A week ago, I wasn't sure she'd even be alive right now. Tonight, she sits at our kitchen table in Atlanta. Sipping tea from a pink floral mug. Wrapped in my favorite silky robe like a warm cocoon. She doesn't say much. Her eyes just track the room and the conversation. She's smiling. She's here. She's come through the worst of it.

From one angle, it seems like a miracle. From another, it's the most natural thing in the world.

Maybe healing isn't something that strikes suddenly. Maybe it grows from the inside, quiet and steady, like roots remembering how to hold and be held. Just this. A soft robe. A cup of tea. A welcome place for Mama at our family table, finally.

Ruth — 2000

ealing isn't linear. It doesn't announce itself with fanfare or follow a tidy arc. It enters sideways through unexpected flyers on bulletin boards in safe places, through radiant hands pressed into broken spines, through baby food passed between generations.

It shows up in a rented duplex, a wheelchair surrounded by thick carpet, a song you don't know the words to, but can't help but sing anyway. Healing shows up even when you don't believe in it. Especially then. This is the part of the story where the house starts to breathe easier, for a while. The porch light flickers on. I curl close. Jen rests, for a moment, in Mama's house shaped by sheer will.

Before this became a story about coming home, it was about learning how to leave. Let's go back. Not to sparkling baseboards or our Alabama beach retreat. Not yet. Let's return to the cracked foundation. To when Jen was still learning how to be herself. Or many selves. Everything feels impossible. Until it doesn't.

Inside The Dream Maker, the only metaphysical shop in Huntsville, Jen breathes easier. Lavender, nag champa, and sacred white sage curl in the air. Tarot decks line the counter like ancient keys. Handmade jewelry fashioned with all kinds of crystals and stones patiently sit inside glass displays cabinets waiting to be picked.

Books on Wicca, Buddhism, and spiritual wisdom lean together. Chakra candles glow in rainbow order. The owners don't mind if she hangs around for hours, wandering among singing bowls and possibilities. Reading books. It's the only place in town that doesn't ask her to explain herself. Ever since Dad ran away with his tail between his legs back to California and the epic collapse of their family agreement, Jen comes here to catch her breath. To find the part of her that trusts her own wisdom. She's not gonna let Dad's stupid ass decisions get in the way of owning that wisdom.

The betrayal is so complete, she can't even say goodbye. She breaks into his brokedown rental trailer, and rescues the little weenie dog he can't take care of. She declares quite matter of factly to Dad who slumps on the couch, "He's mine now."

He doesn't argue. Sometimes saving a life means taking back what should've never been left in the first place. Especially if it's a dog. Especially if it's part of yourself.

At the back of The Dream Maker, a flyer tacked to a bulletin board catches her eye: *Become an Ordained Interfaith Minister.*

A year-long program led by a circle of elder women— The Alliance of Divine Love.

She stares at the flyer for a long time. It doesn't feel strange, more like recognition. Something inside her says, *of course.* Interfaith makes sense. She's always been drawn to explore her mind and heart. Buddhist books in one hand, self-help books in the other. Crystals tucked in her pocket for good luck and healing. Brightly beaded hemp necklaces with blown glass pendants. She loves them. All of it. She finds truth in all of it. All that is good and rooted in love, she believes in that. She doesn't know if she understands love. Not fully. But she wants to. She's always wanted to. She scribbles the number down from the flyer on a borrowed piece of receipt paper. Folds it, puts it in her pocket, keeps it there for a few days.

Then one afternoon, she picks up the phone.

"Hello, Rhonda?"

The voice on the other end is warm. Real. Something deep in Jen exhales. She signs up within minutes of the phone call and starts on the path to become a minister. Not to become someone else. Not to be a healer. Not to be whole. Just to be closer to love. Close to the love she believes she missed out on. To remember that she already belongs to love. This community of mentors, healers, and mystics provides nourishing care, a safe, steady replacement for the loss of Dad.

She showed up every other week, eight of them in a circle, each with some ache they were trying to turn into light. Rhonda led the group with laughter and listening, they sat together, barefoot in a small room that smelled like incense and a new opportunity.

They read the workbooks. Shared their experiences. Did homework. Practiced stillness. They learned to ask questions that didn't need answers right away. The mantra woven through everything was *"In the highest degree of love."* That's what they were training in. Not belief. Not dogma. Not perfection. Just love in its fullest expression.

Rhonda said, "Let love do the work. Trust that."

Jen? She was still unsure. Just trying to move towards the light in her own way, still stitched with self-doubt. But I could feel something happening. The beginning of coming home.

At Athens State, Jen makes the Honor Roll, despite constant math struggles. She never finished 10th grade, she did get that GED she promised Mama. Despite a collapsing spine and all the years lost to chaos, she shines in school.

At twenty-eight, she's older than most of her classmates,

her humor disarms everyone. She's the one cracking jokes in class, helping people feel less weird, less alone. She can connect with anyone, that's one of her gifts.

Art classes. Psychology. Religion. Ceramics. She eats it all up. Learning lights her up from the inside like someone plugged her into her own life for the first time. People feel it. Professors lean in. Classmates ask her to study together. She's not just surviving anymore, she's building something. Her life. Her mind. A self that makes sense separate from Dad, the last person she wants to be like.

For the first time, she's living inside a story that feels like her own. She feels the comeback in her bones. It shows in the way she moves through campus, slowly, carefully, one aching step at a time, but upright. Proud. Alive. We're tall as the trees now. Look how far we've come!

Frannie storms rage on. Now fourteen, the rage hits hard. Literally. More physically. Hormones turn the volume up on everything. Jen can't hold her safely, those old basket holds that Dad taught don't work anymore. Frannie's stronger now. Jen's spine collapses more and more.

Fannie says, "I hope I paralyze you." And she means it.

Jen still shows up. Still trying. She wants to understand her violent outbursts. She doesn't give up. Not once. But a hard, barely speakable truth begins to emerge, slow and awful: it may not be safe to keep her at home. Even love has limits. Devotion has boundaries. She needs a safety net. For both of them. She assures herself: You're not failing. You're taking care of her. With everything you've got. Even when it hurts. Especially then.

On top of everything else, Jen's body won't stop unraveling. Her snake-curved spine squeezes tight on her lungs. She wheezes climbing stairs at school. Pain is a baseline underneath everything, low, steady, inescapable.

She keeps on keeping on anyway. She always does, but it's getting harder to pretend everything is okay. Jen doesn't have insurance and can't afford the cash price for an appointment to see an orthopedic doctor.

Then, a stroke of grace. She's accepted into a charity care program at a university hospital in nearby Birmingham. A consultation. That's all it's supposed to be, but it's really a portal. The surgeon is blunt: "We can help you. Fix your back and deal with those compression fractures. But it's radical."

Spinal reconstruction. A Luque construct. Metal rods straight up the spine, from stem to stern. Total fusion. She'll never twist or bend her back again. She'll need to learn to walk again, the doctor says. The University hospital offers to pay for everything, since she's a student, she qualifies for a charity care program. She says yes. Sometimes when the pain becomes louder than fear, you'll say yes to anything to shut it up.

In the freezing pre-op bay, lit by harsh fluorescents and warmed by a stack of thin heated blankets, Jen twists slowly left, then slowly right. Cracks the vertebrae in her spine one last time. A farewell: goodbye, old body.

She doesn't cry. She just breathes. She's an old pro at being a patient, resigned to this radical Hail Mary move to keep her walking and relieve the constant pain.

I gnaw at her guts, claw the walls of our ribcage, but she can't hear me. Not over the roar of what's coming.

Lamar arrives into the pre-op room where she's waiting. Steady. Glowing. Our blue-eyed angel. He's a lighthouse though every storm. Mama never comes to the hospital to visit, says it's too triggering.

"You'll be fine, Darlin'. I'll be here when you wake up."

Nine hours later, she wakes. The pain is different now—sharper, cleaner, brutal in a whole new way. Two rods run the length of her spine. Alien scaffolding holding her upright. They stand her up the very next day, perched in the center of a circular walker that encompasses her freshly filleted body like a metal corset. They say getting up after major spine surgery is important, she tries to meet that goal. To stand upright. But standing is excruciating. The reality of this new life crushes her spirit. Breathing is easier now. The old curve is gone, but so is everything she knew about how to move in the world.

She starts from zero. In rehab, she relearns it all: how to sit up without falling over, log rolls to get out of bed, because rods don't bend, how to stand without tipping, how to trust her legs again. Nothing is automatic. Every motion requires focus, precision, and lots of surrender. She cries all the time. Gets frustrated. Grieves her old spine, as she starts to belong to this new one.

Then, a bright spot: A teenage girl, Becky, with Spina Bifida, is assigned to the bed next to hers in the rehab hospital, she's recovering from surgery too. They hit it off instantly with the same dark humor, the same craving for fries, pudding cups, and distractions.

Becky's mom visits daily, gentle-voiced and steady. She brings snacks and soft encouragement to both of them. Jen soaks it in. Every "You're doing great, sweetheart" lands exactly where it needs to.

She and the girl speed through the hospital in power wheelchairs, with its maze of skywalks, they carve a golden path of their own. Cookies in hand. Five pudding cups, chocolate and vanilla. Burgers on their laps. Loud, unapologetic laughter slicing through sterile hospital life.

The hospital cafeteria becomes their kingdom and primary destination. Not only because it's grand, with literally everything you could want to eat. Not only because it's all free. Also because in that brightly-lit pocket of the world, they aren't patients. They aren't stories people pity. They're two humans finding joy, wheeling forward, together towards healing.

Rhonda visits with the ministers from The Alliance of Divine Love, it eases the loneliness and sting of Mama not coming. They lay hands on Jen and flood her full of Reiki healing light.

Back home, Frannie keeps spiraling. Her outbursts escalate. She kicks a police officer at school and is expelled. There's no pause button. No time to hope things will settle down on their own.

Frannie is committed to the Wallace Center, an institution already under investigation for multiple suspicious deaths. Jen does her research. Reads the reports. Feels the floor tilt and threaten to swallow them both whole. It's a bad place. Frannie can't stay there. She's not staying there if Jen has anything to do with it.

Fresh from spinal surgery, barely able to move, lift, sleep, or care for herself in any meaningful way, she still shows up. Rolls into that state-mandated meeting like a raptor—perched in her Quickie wheelchair, sharp-eyed, relentless. She brings records. Printouts of possibilities. Pictures of Frannie over time. Lots and lots of context. She wants them to see her as a person, a real person with real history and a real life beating heart.

She speaks clearly, fiercely, she knows what happens to disabled folks in systems that stop seeing them as human beings. She doesn't stop. Not until Frannie gets placed somewhere else. The state acquiesces. They'll give her a waiver to pay for a spot at a group home. It's not perfect but it's safe. It's not the Wallace Center. Anyplace except that house of horrors.

It's not a dream. It's not a nightmare either. A group home is its own stable ground—its own kind of dignity. For now, that's enough.

By 2003, Jen's out of the chair and walking again. She graduated with a Bachelor's degree from Athens State. Her aunt, practical and no-nonsense, just like Mama, offers to take her to Paris as a gift. On the plane, somewhere over the Atlantic, her aunt looks over quite earnestly and asks if she hopes to meet a man while in France.

Jen doesn't flinch. "I'm already in a relationship," she says enthusiastically. "With a woman!"

Silence. It's pretty clear her Aunt doesn't approve of queer love. She doesn't ask anything else. Just opens a magazine and moves on. Silence.

Jen holds her truth close to heart. Quiet and steady. It's something she doesn't need to justify. And Paris? Paris is magic.

Crème brûlée three ways. Queer bookstores tucked behind ivy-covered alleys. Frida at the Pompidou. She reads butch-femme erotica locked away in the bathtub of their shared hotel room, lust, language, and light spilling through the small window over her. She daydreams of her woman back home, the one who lives high up on the mountain. For a little while, it feels like everything might be possible.

But that mountain is hard to climb. So are relationships when you've only ever known yourself through the lens of survival. The woman breaks up with her not long after she returns home from Paris. It's a heartbreak. It's hard for love to stay when Jen's busy pushing everyone away.

In 2004, a rod broke. It starts with a strange click. A sudden jolt in her lower back. A metallic alien clicking dialect no human wants to understand. The pain sharpens. Worsens. Won't let go. She instinctively knows that sound, knows exactly what it means. She can't walk.

X-rays confirm, the hardware snapped. A second surgery is scheduled. She barely has time to adjust, before she's back on the operating table, hoping this time the fusion will hold. She wants to believe the worst is over.

But it isn't. Two more rods break not long after. This time, the surgeon offers a third operation, a more total fusion that includes her pelvis.

"It's the only way," he says.

She nods, and agrees to more surgery. Not because she feels brave. Not because she knows the right things to do. But because, what choice is there? Her spine is literally breaking. She's tired of always collapsing. Her life feels like one big breakdown. She says yes. Again.

The butch dyke she's dating at the time is a psych nurse with more red flags than a protest rally. They offer to move in temporarily to help with recovery. Jen's post-surgery, not able to twist or lift, or move her pelvis at all, so she says yes. It's not perfect, but she needs help.

They make all the right promises:

"I've got you."

"You won't have to lift a finger."

"You just focus on healing."

For a few weeks, it worked. They coexist. There are meds. Bowls and bowls of cereal. Silence. Jen tries not to notice the tension building up like steam behind the walls.

One morning she's up and out of bed, transferring

herself into the chair alone and wheeling into the living room through a thick ocean of carpet. From the radiator vent, she hears a voice. She thinks she recognizes it, but can't tell if she's hallucinating from the Fentanyl patch they gave her, or if it's actual voices she's hearing.

A whisper. Then another. "What are you wearing?"

Those words are not for her. They're for someone else. The butch dyke is cheating. With an ex. From the basement. In her house. Oh hell no!

Jen pushes herself to the door at the top of the basement stairs, hips aching, heart furious. She doesn't hesitate. She doesn't hold back. Not unlike Mama, she knows how to throw some devastating verbal grenades of her own.

"Get out! Get the fuck out of my house, you piece of shit!"

Just like that, the Butch Dyke is gone. No excuses. No goodbye.

Jen's on her own again. No partner. No caretaker. Just Jen. Just me, deep inside, watching. Waiting. Mama and Lamar help when they can, rides to appointments, hot meals dropped off when they have time. Most days, it's cereal, and pushing her wheelchair through that unforgiving carpet, one slow roll at a time.

This is what survival looks like when the bottom keeps falling out, but you still refuse to disappear. Weeks go by. The house is quiet. Jen with her weenie dogs who piss on the old carpet. Pushing through pain and loneliness. Days in bed blur together. She's surviving, just barely. Her body's wrecked. Her spirit's thin as a dollar.

Then, one day, a friend from the queer community reaches out. "I know someone who might have some ideas for your floors," she says. "She's in Atlanta. She's kind,

practical, and doesn't flake. Want me to ask if she'll come?"
Jen shrugs. Sure. Why not? She doesn't expect anything. No
miracles. Just a little help would be nice.

Saturday morning, there's a knock at the door. And
there she is. Iris. Hoodie. Jeans. Candy apple red shoes that
shine like a promise. Jen's knees would've buckled at first
sight if she could stand. Iris is incredibly handsome, a perfect smile, spiked silver hair, she's twelve years older than
Jen. She's driven a good long way to get there, from Atlanta
to Huntsville. Just to help, because she said she would. She
walks into that duplex like she's been there a hundred times.
Like it's no big deal. But it is. A very big deal. No small talk.
No ego. Just sleeves rolled up, tool belt on, ready to work.

The first weekend she tears up the carpet. That heavy,
binding, pissy mess that's been keeping Jen trapped. Iris rips
it out like it's nothing. For Jen it feels a lot like a miracle. The
next weekend she sands the floor. The weekend after that
she stains it mahogany brown. She always brings lunch. And
dinner. Does everything possible to make Jen's life easier.
Pays for everything. Returns the next weekend. The one
after that. Always driving. Always showing up. Always bringing gifts and anything to make Jen smile.

It's almost too good to be true. I don't trust it, but I watch.
I watch Iris show up. I watch her work hard, another stranger
coming into our lives, changing it for the better. I watch her
bring order to our mess. At first, I pace. Ears high. Chest
tight. Waiting for another letdown. She doesn't flinch when
the pain gets loud. Doesn't run when Jen's past surfaces. She
leans in. She listens. She never turns away.

Iris. Kind, steady, right-on-time Iris. They hold hands in
the car. Talk about nothing and everything. The world feels
different with her in it. Softer. More alive. Jen starts to breathe

differently. Starts to imagine things. Romantic things.

She's falling for Iris, quietly, steadily, from one week-end to the next. They text like teenagers. Email long, tender reflections back and forth. Their connection is electric and old, like they'd already met in another life and this was just a reunion.

Jen flirts. Then sends a love letter, honest and a little scared. Iris replies: "You're too young. But you need to find someone. Like me."

How confusing! Still, Iris keeps coming back. Like clock-work, moving on to paint her bedroom walls bright pink with a touch of gold glitter. Jen's healing more and more. Their bond deepens. Not flashy. Just *real*. So very real. Like old soul friends coming together again.

One Sunday morning, Jen offers Iris her sticky hand covered in applesauce. Grinning. Teasing. "Now you're sticky too." They never stop calling each other that: Sticky. Sticky Forever.

In 2006, news came that Dad was dying from sepsis, he'd been pushing hard drugs. His decline was rapid. There's no time to spare, Iris doesn't hesitate and buys Jen a plane ticket. She handles the details so Jen can fall apart, a pattern that will be repeated again and again over time.

Jen and Big Brother fly to California, separately. They haven't shared space in years. Not since they were angry teenagers. Now they share a hotel room. Two grown adults who've lived a thousand lives in between. There's tension, yes. There's equally a peacefulness. A kind of truce that forms when you both realize you've made it through the same nightmare in different ways.

In the hospital room, they say the all words that need to be said to Dad:

Thank you.
I forgive you.
I love you.

Doctors in the critical care unit are adamant that he can't be touched, he's contagious with infectious bugs they say. Full protective gowns and gloves form the final barrier between Dad and his kids. A gentle Indian nurse adjusts the morphine. She speaks softly, like she's done this a hundred times, but still means it.

"It's okay to go, Papa. Your babies are here now."

Dad dies in peace. Not in a ditch. Not in jail. Not alone. Not forgotten. He leaves his body loved, forgiven.

The next day, the two heartsick siblings retrace old stomping grounds. Drive past those city bus stops they used to wait at in the dark. The Denny's they took the city bus to, all by themselves for Thanksgiving dinner, when Mama was too sick to get out of bed. They traced the bus route to and from the hospital they still remembered by heart. They tried to make sense of their lives and the journey to this moment.

They stop at the old house, the one stretched to hold so much screaming, so much betrayal, and some Happy Meals too. It used to feel huge, like the whole universe could fit inside that house.

Now? It looks impossibly small. Shrunken with time. Warped by memories. Still, some parts of their lives are folded into those walls forever. Maybe someone living there still hears the screams. Dad is still right there on the couch talking to the TV.

Big Brother returns home, synchronistically he lives within 30 minutes from Iris in Georgia. Jen decides to stay a few more days in California. She needs space. Time to breathe. A distraction to wipe the steam of grief from her field of vision.

She makes plans to meet up with old friends, some new ones. Wanders through familiar streets in the Bay Area that still feel like portals. Smiles at the old 7-11, eats pizza at their favorite place. She's filled with grief and relief, a strange mix of paradoxical feelings.

Back in the hotel room, alone, lonely, full of ache, she picks up the phone and calls Iris.

"I might go on a date while I'm here," she says, casually, chest full of butterflies.

She knows what she wants. She just doesn't know if she's allowed to want it. She hopes Iris will stop her. There's a long pause.

Iris is out walking the gorge, breathing heavy from the uphill climb. Then, finally, half exasperated, half tender:

"What do you want from me, Sticky?"

Jen's voice is steady, steady like it's been her whole life when she recognizes the destiny she knows is hers.

"I want you to tell me not to go. I want you to tell me to come home. And be with you. Forever."

Another pause. Longer this time.

It feels like the sky could split open in that silence. Then Iris says, soft and sure:

"Don't go, Sticky. Come home. Be with me."

Jen flies back to Atlanta the next day. Their first kiss is at the airport. Messy. Beautiful. Not a fairy tale happy ending. This is something much better. Not a match made in heaven. A match made in the wreckage. Sure and steady. Fire and gold. Sanded floors. Smooth rides. Gentle hand holds. Safe ground. We're not starting over. We're beginning again. This time, our house will hold.

Ruth on the State of Things

Humans get disconnected in all kinds of ways.
Not just from each other,
but from themselves,
from the inner house they're meant to live in.
They wander their own halls with the lights off,
forgetting which rooms hold joy,
which ones hold pain,
and which are just dusty with waiting.
But the disconnection doesn't stop there.
It stretches outward,
into breath, into body, into instinct.
Into relationships.
Into the more-than-human world.
Into Earth, our shared home.
Now here we are: the Anthropocene.
A word that sounds like a fancy sandwich,
but is actually the name for this age of unraveling.
Your unraveling.
Our unraveling.
An era where human brilliance becomes a wrecking ball.
So much ingenuity.
So little reverence.
I'll be honest with you:
It's a mess.
And I say that as a dog.
We eat our own shit!
Even I can tell, this path we're on isn't sustainable.
In the scramble to become gods,

humans forgot you were animals first.
Born of Earth.
Breath-makers.
Water-bearers.
Dreamers under the same sky as owls and opossums.
You forgot how to howl.
How to root.
How to be with silence without trying to fill it.
You forgot we live in a shared house.
Not just your inner one—
which, yes, needs tending, mending,
sometimes a full-on gut renovation—
but the bigger one.
The planetary one.
Our planet, she's alive.
She breathes.
Every living being is a room in her great, beating house.
If you stop tending your part,
your room,
it doesn't just collapse on you,
it collapses on all of us.
Still, I believe there's hope.
Because you are not a single self,
doomed to repeat the same worn out patterns.
You are a constellation.
A council.
A wildly creative committee of inner parts,
each with its own wisdom, its own wound,
its own longing to be seen, to be met.
You are not a monolith.
You are not stuck.
You are multiplicity,
waiting to be remembered.

That old myth about being one fixed identity?
Compost.
Thank the Earth for that.
Even researchers are catching up
to what the mystics always knew:
Self isn't set in stone.
It's a river made of many stones.
Here's where it really gets good:
the more conscious you become of your many selves,
the more you realize your wholeness.
The more you see wholeness in everything.
The more easily your river flows.
That's healing.
That's alchemy.
Not fixing what's broken—
but finding the gold in the cracks.
Every part of you belongs.
Every version matters.
Even the one who barks too loud,
or knocks things over in excitement.
Don't be so linear.
Being linear is what got us into this pickle.
We're not flattening anymore.
We're digging deep.
Reaching inward.
You're not just a hallway.
You're the whole damn house.
Some rooms need airing out.
Some are locked.
Some are wild jungles of feeling.
There are whole libraries of knowledge inside you.
Some parts are being renovated.

Some doors deserve to stay closed.
And if the lights are off in some of your rooms?
It's never too late to turn them back on.
Ask yourself:
Who's home today?
What needs feeding?
What part needs rest?
What wants to be let out to run in the yard
and roll in something weird and stinky?
Tend your inner house.
Not just for you.
For all of us.
Because the more humans come home on the inside,
the more you remember:
you belong to Earth,
not above it.
That kind of remembering?
It changes things.
It makes space for reciprocity to grow.
For repair.
For reverence.
You don't have to come home all at once.
But please, be on your way.
Even one pawstep is enough.

— *Ruth*

Chapter 8:

Bearing

Jen — Winter 2022

Monday morning, Mama and I head back to Alabama after a wonderful visit to Georgia celebrating Frannie's birthday. The sky is clear, and thankfully, traffic is light. Mama made it through our trip without a single emergency. Frannie was radiant, thirty-five and happy. Both legit miracles in their own right.

There were years when I didn't know if we'd make it. When I first met Frannie, she was an angry little girl. A heart on fire, burning with rage that had every reason to exist. When she got mad, she kicked shins, sometimes bit down on my skin hard enough to draw blood. She punched me until the tears came. Touch was never soft with her, at least not at first. She couldn't tolerate hugs, only the firm grip of basket-holds when her body lost control. For a long time, that was the only kind of touch she could bear, containment, not comfort.

Now she welcomes comfort. Laughs easily. Dances with glee. Remembers birthdays. Shows genuine care. Seeks out hugs. She takes care of who and what she loves in her own ways. Her healing isn't accidental. It's the result of every hard choice I made to fight for her future, even when mine was falling apart. It's the outcome of Mama and Lamar's love and care for us all those years. Maybe her healing is my healing, too. My healing is hers. A living thread in this lineage of love that we've been weaving together. Not perfectly. But with everything we've got. Without a doubt strengthened by Iris' steady commitment, love, and care.

I nervously glance over at Mama, then out at the highway, then back again before asking, oh so carefully, "Do ya think you'll be able to take care of yourself if I go home Friday?"

I'm not trying to push her. I just need to know. I gotta get back to our pack. To rest. To reset. To breathe. To my surprise, she doesn't hesitate. "Oh, I think so... I'm feeling better every day."

We ride most of the way back in silence. Not our usual hard quiet, the air seems more peaceful now.

Maybe we've really turned a corner. We've been here before—things looking up, then the floor crumbling beneath us. This time, I feel something different. A subtle shift. Strength in Mama. The tiniest click of gears engaging on the way to better health. She's made it through a whole lot in one lifetime. If anyone has what it takes for a comeback, it's her. She's the toughest bird I know.

Me? I'm gonna keep showing up for her. Proving I'm a

safe place. I'm still gonna be me. Not perfect—just present. Here. I was so loud as a baby, I came into the world scream-ing. I was instantly an unsafe place for Mama, who was aller-gic to my screams. I'm aiming to be a different kind of safe house now. Yah, I'm still loud. Yah, Mama still grabs her ears when I laugh too loud or criticize too much all these years later. I can't fix everything. I can't make her see me differ-ently. Love me differently. I don't want to. I can't change her mind. But, I can and I will hold my light steady while she heals. The worms are out of the can about the condition of her house. About how hard things have been for her. Might as well make peace with those worms.

Worms, after all, are alchemists, you know. They wiggle through rot and make it fertile. Blindly. Turn decay into healthy soil, quietly, without complaint.

There's a lot of wisdom in that. We don't need eyes to sense what's true. We don't have to be perfect to start over again. Just move through the mess.

With monthly visits, Ruth's help, Mama doing her part as she gets stronger, I believe we can keep this house uplifted. Keep it alive. More honest. More held. More seen.

She's coming back to life. You'll see. Feisty and back to being full of life in no time!

When Dad died, there was a strange relief tangled up in that grief. In death, he felt safe for me to love again. Safe to have a relationship with. That relationship I wanted with him, that I craved more than anything so much of my life, I enjoy that connection with him now. He answers my calls, just a little more cosmically now.

When Lamar died, and then years later my father-in-law died, I grieved their loss hard. Missed them like I lost my own limbs. I was also relieved they weren't suffering anymore. But this whole ordeal, Mama almost dying, this was something else. It cracked open something primal in me. My body lit up with the panic of an electrical storm. It felt like I was gonna die without her. Maybe, in some small way, I would.

When a Mama dies, part of the child dies too. When a child dies, part of the Mama goes with them. Love never dies. It just shifts form. It becomes raw radiant potential. It becomes a promise, the promise of love is in rebirth. I believe Mama and I will find each other again when she dies. When I die. We'll find each other in every realm. Over and over. In every form we take. Our love is stubborn like that.

When we arrive back at Mama's house in Alabama, I help her inside. Settle the little dogs. Turn the heat on, then head down the highway to pick up the big dogs at the vet. The reunion is pure joy, snouts nuzzling, tails thudding, paws dancing. Happy to be home. Even Lily, who didn't get adopted after all, is over the moon. She belongs here. They all do. This is mama's family and they need each other.

Mama? She didn't come home with that feeding tube. That's the biggest miracle.

I've been scheming ways to make life easier for Mama. I've got an idea, but I'm holding off till after her procedure to remove a kidney stone on Tuesday. No need to make things harder while I'm trying to make things easier.

Meanwhile, I watch the dogs sniff their way through their new fenced yard. Mama rests, sitting in the backyard in a peeling teal lawn chair, face tilted to the sun like one of her flowers trying to open to the light.

"I just can't believe this fence," she says with a smile. "Lamar and I always talked about doing it. Never happened. It's a miracle. Everything you did—it's all a miracle."

Then she gets up and starts tinkering in her garden. Tending to her babies buried in pots. Waking up dirt with spells kept in her twisted-root fingers. As much as she's needed the darkness these last few months, I feel the light nourishing her now. Her body lifts, just slightly, that's how I know: she's gonna bloom again. It's a real privilege to witness a flower unfurl in its own time and space.

Later that week, the new gutter was installed. Another big checkmark. The house kinda glows now. Light comes in easier. Warmth rises through the vents. There's this unmistakable hum in the air, the sound of possibility. That's the kind of magic she needs. That's the kind I believe in.

Tuesday, she has an outpatient procedure under anesthesia. The doctor takes out a big honkin' kidney stone. I don't know how much that contributed to her decline, but getting it out feels like an exclamation point at the end of our very long sentence.

When we get home, she falls into a deep sleep. She's almost ready to be on her own. Me? I'm feeling this weird ache of not wanting to leave. I'm so worried about her. Sad to leave a place I never even wanted to be in.

Well, isn't that weird?

The Huntsville city limit sign used to crash over me like a wave of shame. I came here only when I had to. I avoided it. Partly because of the memories. Partly because, maybe on some level I knew Mama needed more from me. Something I didn't yet know how to give. Something she wasn't ready to let me give.

Here we are. She's healing. I'm healing. Her house is transformed. All the money donated is being put to good use to help Mama thrive. It was a one-time outpouring, one we will never forget.

Me? Us. We feel... aligned.

None of it happened alone.

The Roberts Family.

Bill Hill.

The Marines.

Aurelio.

Miguel.

Liz.

The kind folks who contributed to Mama's GoFundMe.

Iris.

Frannie.

Earthbound angels, every single one. People who didn't look away. People who said yes. Synchronicity moving through them, through us, like lightning. All the folks who helped our family? They're cut from that same cloth of kindness that's been shown to us again and again by strangers my whole life. Not a rescue. No pity. Just the steady hands of strangers showing up when we needed them. A guiding thread of care, pulled throughout time. That's alchemy, transforming a breakdown into a breakthrough. Loneliness into love. A crumbling house into a safe place.

Mama and Lamar's house is part of my healing too. I belong to this land. To the birds. The mountains. They always remind me: this isn't just the place where you fell apart, it's also where you came together. .

Yep, this place raised you up, too. That mountain always had your back.

Mama's love wasn't soft, but it was steadfast in its own way. Brillo pad love: abrasive and practical. Hard enough to scrape raw, but somehow still rooted in an odd kind of care. There's a kind of love that shows up, raggedy and misfiring, but it tries. That's the kind we had. Our stories aren't nice, neat, or gentle, but they're still about showing up, sometimes in ways we wish we didn't have to. Often in ways that saved each other. Every generation, smoothing the edges of our family lines. Big Brother is doing that work with his girls, my brilliant nieces, filled with their birthright gift of a safe, stable, and nurturing childhood. Raised in a home where gifts and talents are celebrated. Something we never had.

Frannie and I are still tangling and untangling our roots. We've been on a long journey of learning what it means to be held without conditions. We don't need to earn what should've always been ours, safety within ourselves, and with each other. We're committed to being safe places for each other.

Iris, our steady, faithful Iris, she's poured love into us for seventeen years. The kind of love that doesn't flinch. The kind that stays. These are our loops of love, imperfect, but enduring.

Iris is our forever home.

Ruth strums my heartstrings, the familiar thrum of my protector who never stops keeping watch.

Getting lost turned out to be a good way to get found?

I used to think I was lost. Slipped out of my life like a ghost through drywall. But what I called "lost" was actually space, a widening of sorts that led to an unlit hallway where something vital was trying to speak. Trying to get my attention. To get me to remember my light. Ruth was always there.

I thought I was cut off from myself. Turns out I was just curled up in a closet. Hiding under a pile of coats on a dusty chair no one had sat in for years. I was never lost. Never broken. I was just tucked away inside myself for safe keeping.

Slowly, breath by breath, I unfolded over the years. I didn't have to force my way back into the world. I only had to listen. To wait. To let the rooms remember me, so that I could remember that I am a house. I never left my house, I've been here all along. Now, I claim it, clear as day: I belong here. To this life. To Iris and Frannie. To my body as it is. I belong to me, to this house, to my circle of selves.

"Mama," I ask softly, "What do you think about me and Iris taking two of the little dogs to live with us in Atlanta?"

She studies me like a hawk circling something squirming helpless on the ground. Then shrugs. "If Iris is okay with it, I'm okay with it."

Just like that. Two fewer dogs to manage. Two more loves joining our pack. By week's end, I'm packing my suitcase. I leave a few things in my room, on the shores of Fantasy Island. I'll be back soon enough.

Iris is coming to pick me up, I've been using Mama's car this whole time. This is the end of one chapter and the beginning of something new. The house, my house, her house, our house, has changed.

So have we, you know?

We're closer, wouldn't you say?

Yep.

I'm proud.

Me too.

I don't yet have words for all of it. But this I know:

We let you in. Into our house. Into our lives. Into rooms we'd kept hidden— closets full of miracles, harsh truths, and family secrets. We showed you our cracked foundations so you'd know: this is normal too. It's okay to clean things up. Make things better inside. This is the alchemy of being a house: letting darkness do its sacred work. Inviting the light in, in whatever way it comes. Allowing others inside. Learning how to stay. Becoming our own safe place. A home, finally at last.

This is how we live. This is how we become. This is how we are made new, again and again.

"I love you, Mama, super much. I'll see you soon."

I step outside and close Mama's door behind me—not just to her house, but to our old arrangements. The roles I perfected and protected so our lives wouldn't fall apart. Those scripts I memorized as a kid. Her moods I tracked like storms on the horizon.

She did the best she could with what she had. So did I. We stayed too long in costumes that no longer fit. Held on when we needed to let go. Let go when maybe we should've held on.

I'm not performing anymore. I'm not who she needed me to be, who she wanted me to be, never was. That's okay.

I'm who I need me to be now. I'm the one I needed. I'm the one I was looking for. No more shrinking or stretching to fit inside anyone else's story. I don't carry the weight of anyone's disappointment.

I'm walking away from Mama's house with everything that's mine: My life. My stories. My messy healing. Me—as I am, a living house of many rooms. One soul born of many parts.

I spent so much of my life looking for home, but it was never lost. It's always been here, in the stillness, in the breakdown, in every version of me. Then. Now. Still becoming.

Ruth — 2011

There's a moment when you've carried so much, for so long, that the load doesn't disappear, it just shifts. Those bags you dragged through every doorway are finally set down. For the first time, you look around and realize: I'm not in a holding pattern anymore, I'm home. I'm a living home. It's a mind blowing transformation.

This is that moment. A return that doesn't erase what came before, but braids it in. Love that doesn't fix, but holds. Selves that don't stray, but stay. Our house isn't just the wreckage. Jen's no longer trying to survive it. It took a whole lifetime to get here. A whole rotating choir of selves. A mother, still healing. A daughter, thriving. A partner, faithful as spring. A voice within—my voice— once all bark and warning, now humming steady and ready like a hearth fire.

This isn't the end of our story. It is where something old and heavy gets laid down. The weight of proving, lifted. The ache of being unseen, witnessed. Something simpler, more natural blooms. A knowing. A truth. A remembering. A homecoming. The beginning of the life we always wanted.

To understand how far we've come, we return, one last time, down into the part of the house that taught us how to be a home.

When Jen and Iris got married in 2008 in at the Palace of Fine Arts in San Francisco, it was the best day of their lives. Love had been unfolding between them since that first door opened—red sneakers, sawdust, sweet, sweet Sticky Love. It was love that saw through her layers. Through a constant need to perform. Love showed Jen her own reflection, not as the train wreck she always believed herself to be, as someone with potential. Trustworthy. Worthy.

More than anything, she wanted to match that reflection. To love herself the way Iris loved her. To believe in herself the way Iris believed in her. The gap between Jen and her own self-love felt like a gaping void. If she stared into that black hole too long, she'd fall right in. Or die entirely.

So, that's what she did. Symbolically, anyway.

One day not long after their wedding, she moves the furniture again. She knows it's not safe for her body. She knows Iris asked her not to. Promised even. But she slides the couch anyway. Lifts a heavy potted plant. "I didn't lift anything," she'll say. "I only slid things."

But Iris sees it all. The rearranged layout. Tiny betrayals.

"You said you'd wait." Iris snaps back mad.

Jen folds inward, ashamed, angry, raw, bolts to the backyard. When people do bad things they get kicked out of the house, that's what she remembers anyway.

Towel still wrapped around her wet body, feet shoved into sherpa boots without socks, she hides from Iris in an area beside the house in the backyard.

There's a house above, and a house below. The one above is filled with light, warmth, her wife, her dogs. The life she built, and the future they're shaping together. The one below is the crawlspace: dark, tight, packed with cold earth. The part of her that always believed she was too broken to belong. She chooses the one below.

She presses her body hard into the dirt. Birds overhead go quiet. She's possessed by grief. By frustration. By the deep desire to disappear into the dark—"I don't wanna live like this anymore!" She gives in. She goes underground.

Shame convinced her she didn't belong in a house of light. That the pain of her past made her unworthy. She believed she was too broken. That she never belonged. She was destined to be just like Dad, after all. She begged the ground to swallow her. And, mercifully, it did...

I watched as she fell.

Down through topsoil and thick red Georgia clay.

Down through memories. Through sadness.

Through the winding hallways of the many selves she's been.

Down, down, down she fell, until she landed in the root system of trees.

Something slipped away down there.

Not a life, but the masks she wore..

Selves made of proving, pleasing, pretending,

not gone, just finally seen.

That summer, she started a practice. A ritual.

Every morning, blanket-wrapped and barefoot,

she laid down in the backyard beneath two trees who

taught her to listen,
The Riser and The Diver.
That ordinary backyard was transformed into a sanctuary.
The ground became an altar.
Trees turned into wise teachers.
Her body, a doorway.
Her mind, as always, a thunderstorm that raged.
Still, she stayed.
Thoughts swelled and crashed.
Old stories sparked and flared.
She watched them.
Not running.
Just witnessing.
A thought would appear, she'd spot it in her mind.
Then return to the moment, to the trees.
That loop, over and over.
Again and again.
Breath by breath.
That was it. Simple. Profound.

Until the storms softened.
She was shedding old skins.
She stopped performing.
She started, for the first time, to simply be.
The pain didn't disappear,
she noticed she wasn't the pain.
That pain didn't define her.
It was part of her, but definitely not all of her.
Those old mixtapes kept on playing, but suddenly she knew
they weren't her stories.
They were the thoughts and stories of other people.
"Don't believe everything you think," she'd say to herself.

"You are not your thoughts.
That was a return.
Not to somewhere above herself.
Not beneath.
But within.
Going inside wasn't an escape, it was a return.
The trees said her mind was weather. Her thoughts, clouds passing by. Her true self? She was all sky. One day, quietly, miraculously, out of nowhere, she caught a glimpse of her inner sky.
Noticed some space between her thoughts.
There were times she wanted to give up,
When the noise in her mind was unbearable.
She screamed into the dirt, "What the fuck is wrong with me?"
The trees stayed. She stayed too.
She learned to be patient with herself.
Not by force, through presence.
The steady practice of coming home inside, again and again.

Have a thought.
Spot the thought.
Return.
Repeat.
Trees tethered her between worlds.
The same part that once sabotaged, now studied.
She was a scientist of her own consciousness.
A witness to patterns, parts, layers of pain.
She stopped trying to run away from herself.
She started to stay.
In that stillness, in her willingness to stay, something shifted.
A quieting.
Space appeared.

The tiniest glint of awareness between thoughts.
A sliver of something true.
Nothing new, just newly seen.
One morning, late in the summer of that long becoming,
she lay beneath the trees and said,
"If there's anything in me that keeps me from living...take it.
I'm ready now. I wanna live."
And the trees, gentle, steady, loving as they'd been her
whole life, said yes.
Not all at once.
But with the same kindness and care they'd offered since
she was a little girl.
By the hand of grace, she came back to life.
But she didn't come back the same.
She was still Jen,
but she wasn't possessed by those old selves.
She was completely changed,
and no different at all.
The same house, just a home fully inhabited.
She moves differently.
Breathes differently.
She listens.
Asks for help.
Isn't afraid to let love in.
Isn't afraid to stay.

When she moves furniture now,
she does it with Iris.
Together.
Mostly!
She's not alone in this house anymore.
She's not better.

Not fixed.
Just more true.
Integrated.
Aligned.
This is what alchemy looks like.
Not transcendence.
A deep remembering.
Falling apart that becomes falling inward.
Leaving that leads to a homecoming.
Those old selves weren't lost.
They took up space in the floorboards.
In our walls.
In the bones of this house we share.
Now Jen listens when they speak.
She knows which ones to call forward.
Which ones to rest.
The ones want to play.
This too is the alchemy of being a house,
tending our root systems.
Returning home to ourselves,
over and over.
In this house, there's love.
In that love,
there is room for all of us.
My whole circle of selves.
Even parts that wanted to disappear into the crawlspace.
Especially those parts.
Because those parts,
against all odds,
led us home.

Epilogue:

Staying

Spring — 2025

We're sitting at the kitchen table, me and Ruth. Morning light stretches across the floor, warm and familiar. Outside the window, the lake undulates with the activity of fish, turtles, and frogs. Palm trees sway in the breeze like they've got nowhere to be. This is our life now.

Iris is outside, sipping coffee, barefoot as always now that she's retired. We moved to Florida for the weather, for the beauty of it, for the chance to swim more often, which is heaven for my body and The Chronic Pains.

Our newest pup lies just outside the sliding door, black fur with white ticking shining so bright it almost looks blue. His eyes are gold, piercing and exquisite. He was another act of grace in the form of a dog by Mama, she rescued him from the pound just minutes before he was set to be put down. He was picked up as a stray, his name on the sign was Centaur, and she honored that. Half man, half beast, a mythical creature. He was full of heartworms and an enormous amount of love to give. She nursed him through treatment. He's big like Ruth. Watchful. Kind. A ninety pound marshmallow. Way too much dog for Mama to handle. With her permission, Big Brother and I, along with my niece, picked him up, and drove him to Florida to a new life where he could stretch out and stay. We call him Golden, Golden Centaur. He keeps close, trailing us like a shadow. Guarding with quiet loyalty.

That's what we do. That's our job.

The other day, Iris was telling me about a moment with Frannie in the grocery store parking lot. It was one of those bright Florida afternoons where the sun presses its hands over everything, warm and unrelenting.

They were leaving the store, Frannie clutching a few crumpled bills in one hand, two lottery tickets in the other. She'd bought them for me—one dollar each—and was explaining to Iris how much money she had left. She's thirty-eight now, going on thirteen.

Iris, walking beside her, said, "You know what you are now, Frannie?"

"What?"

"A money manager."

Frannie tasted the words on her tongue like a new flavor. "What's that?"

"It's someone who manages their money responsibly."

Frannie lit up, proud as a peacock. "Yeah. I get forty

dollars in allowance this week, and I have eleven now, so that'll make it..." She counted on her fingers, lips moving silently, eyes focused.

"Fifty-one!

"That's right," Iris said.

They walked together, slow and easy, through rows of sunbaked cars. Iris always parks a little farther out, for the steps, the ritual of it. She reminded Frannie that she's not just saving, she's planting seeds for her future. Frannie nodded, serious and proud.

I could picture her exactly, taking it all in, even if the full meaning of being a money manager hadn't fully landed yet. It didn't have to. The pride on her face said everything.

I heard that story secondhand, but I could see it clear as day. A far cry from our harsh beginnings. Our chaos. Our struggle for stability. And here she was, walking in a grocery store parking lot with two lottery tickets and a plan. A Money Manager.

Her growth is a gift of grace. It's the fruit of hard-won love, woven from sweat, stubbornness, and a thousand small acts of believing that we could become more than the world expected, or even allowed, of us. She's not just surviving anymore. She's planning. She's counting. She's thriving.

Pax snores beneath my chair, softly, sweetly. Wicky died almost a year ago. Broke our hearts straight in two. He was the love of our lives. But he visits the way he always trusted most as a blind dog: through the warm sun. We feel him shining on us in the light.

Rudy, one the dogs we asked Mama for, is still here with us, bless him, fifteen years old and slower now, but still smiling every day. The other, Abby passed two years ago, sassy and beloved to the very end. We carried them out of Mama's house, and I like to think we carried them into our next chapter of life right alongside us.

Inside the house, it's quiet enough to hear the ceiling fans tick. The soft hush of our life not rushing anymore. The feeling of finally being in a forever home. I designed every inch of this house when we moved in and renovated—our Sweet Sticky love written all over it.

Big Brother lives nearby in Florida. Still the same in some ways, proud, stoic, always showing up for me, letting me be a baby sister. He's changed too, like we have, no longer the boy wearing shoes too big. Not the teenager who had to disappear to survive. But the man he's become. The dad he's grown into. Sensitive. Fierce. Brilliant. My truest witness. He came home to himself in his own way; I've come home in mine. And these houses, our living houses, are big enough to hold both of us. This is one of many offerings to our generational lines.

We're finding each other again, piece by piece. Part by part. Letting our defenses drop. Remembering what was hard. What was sacred. All that we shared. The way we played. The way we survived. The way we took care of each other the best we could.

Here we are now, two kids inside adult bodies, enjoying deep, soulful conversations. Dinners at the family table. Reflecting on the journey. Laughing together so hard it echoes all the way back to that house of screaming in California. Our love is renovating the walls of that house we shared. Now we get a do-over. A chance to reclaim innocence, this time wrapped in safety and connection.

Ruth is curled up, paws crossed in her usual dignified way. She's a little grayer now. Alert as ever. I guess we both are. But she still looks at me like I'm the center of some very

important map. The kind of gaze that roots me, even when I feel a little unmoored. Especially then.
We made it.

We did.

I trace my fingers along the seam at the table's edge. I didn't know if we would.

Neither did I. But we did. And just making it counts for something.

I nod and look out the window again. A crane lifts from the water with effortless grace. I admire that kind of lightness of being.

It's a good place, isn't it? This home. Our home. It's not just the house. It's you! You're the place.
The home we've been renovating this whole time.

I laugh. Guess we've knocked down a few walls.

Built some too.

There's a pause, not the kind that wants to be filled, but the kind that invites a whole lotta space.
I still have parts I don't understand. Parts that need a lot of attention.

Course you do. You're a house, not a hallway. You don't have to box yourself in all the time.

I close my eyes and let her wisdom settle.
You know what the trees told me?

Everything that matters.

They said I could trust the silence inside me. That I didn't need to fill it. That the spaciousness I was afraid of… was actually sacred. Silence isn't emptiness—it's full of life. That's how it works, the alchemy of being a house. It's born out of silence. Attention. Presence.

It's being brave enough to stay when everything in you wants to run away.

I'm ready for that. That's what I want now, to stay with the things I deserve to stay with. Offer up what I've always longed for, the best of me,—to Iris, to Frannie, Mama, Big Brother, myself, to whatever comes next. Even to Dad, wherever he is in the universe, whatever form he takes.

You're doing it. Just look around. You really are trusting your life.

I am. And I take everything in, the lake, the trees, the ordinary grace of morning. Gentleness. Routine. Belonging.
We moved here when Iris retired. She wanted palm trees. I wanted water, so I can swim—the strongest medicine for my broken body. Frannie wanted to be close to that very famous mouse. We all wanted peace in our own ways, together. We claimed a quiet life with open hands and open hearts. We've been building something soft. Slow. Gentle. A home not just made of walls, but of intention and care.

Every breakdown led me right here. Even Alabama feels different now when I visit. Mama's doing pretty good, still feisty as ever at 80. Still dog sitting for families, and The Roberts Family in Hampton Cove. I fly back every few months to deep clean, clear corners, keep the house seen and humming with care. Mama lets me in now. That may not sound like a miracle to outside observers, but you know it is. For so many years, I wasn't allowed inside.

She welcomes me now. Reluctantly, but she does. I come through that door armed with gloves and sponges, care and conscious attention—a living home within a home within a home. Our relationship tracks much the same: good with distance, not so good when we're together. We try. We give each other lots of space. Mama knows she needs me. I know I need her. That, too, is part of our strange alchemy. Part of this fragile, yet undeniable bond we share.

Ruth noses my leg like she always does. Resting her chin on my knee, breath warm. Just because she lives in me doesn't mean she can't breathe. We've been through a lifetime together, miles of grief, growth, grit, and gratitude. She's more than a voice in my head. She's my companion. A witness. My guide through the darkest times. She's been inside me since the beginning.

I used to think I had to be one right self. Just one perfect thing. Stay trapped in old versions of me.

You tried. Real hard.

I know, I know, I'm the whole damn house! Full of rooms. Full of selves. None of them need to be silenced or evicted.

Even the messy ones.

Especially the messy ones.

Especially me.

I reach inward, deep where she waits, and cup her fuzzy dog face between both hands. She's soft. She's real. She's me.

You were never the problem. You were our perfect, ancient alarm system. I just forgot to reset us once the threats were gone.

I'm glad you remembered. Glad we're not just surviving anymore.

We sat like that for a while. Peaceful. Settled. Nothing dramatic. Just the kitchen table. The lake. Palm trees swaying in the wind. Two old friends sharing this moment of truth, after a very long journey together.

I'm tired a lot. My body hurts all the time.

I know.

I'm happy. I'm so happy. Grateful more than anything to still be alive. But my heart hurts, too. I still have a lot of things to figure out. There's healing to do. I see what's happening, I feel it. The heaviness of our world presses into me—so many are wounded in so many ways.

Houses, both literal and metaphorical, are burning across the map. Some slowly. Some all at once. Our Earth home, along with so many species, are in big trouble. I carry that knowing. That grieving. I don't look away. I stay. In this house. Our house. The one we've built from what was spared, what was salvaged, and what was survived.

I'm not running anymore. Not from the pain of our world. Not from myself. Not from Alabama and everything it represents in my story. I'm lucky to have an incredible therapist for many years who helps me reframe all that heaviness that weighed me down for so long.

There's alchemy in that too, you know?

In what?

Staying. With things that hurt. Not flinching. Not fixing. Not turning away. Just breathing through it. Bearing witness.

I listen, and feel it, her gentle paw, reaching toward me from the inside. I cup it in my hand like it's the most natural thing in the world.

Learning to stay with pain, and someone else's, too. Like Mama. Dad. Making peace with all the people, places, and things we spent our life running from.

I breathe in Ruth's wisdom in a whole lifetime's worth of breath. We sit there, integrated, hand-in-paw. I send thanks to all the selves within us that it took to get us here. Our cracked foundation turned out to be something holy, we are a home built with golden threads of synchronicity. I'm in awe of the weird, wild, wonderful alchemy of it all.

Ruth shifts and rises, her joints a little stiff, tail wagging just the same.

Come on! Let's go play outside. The trees are calling. Life is waiting for us!

I grab my cane and rise, slowly, carefully. Ruth pads toward the door the way she always has, leading just a little ahead of me, but never out of reach.

Family Photo Wall

Baby Jenny

Big Brother & Jen

Big Brother, Dad & Jen

Mama, Frannie & Lamar

Frannie, Iris & Jen

Jen & Mama

A Note On Lived Experience

This isn't a clinical story. It's just a human one. The word alchemy shows up throughout this book, even as part of the title. I'm using it as a way to describe the quiet, powerful changes that happened inside me over time. I know alchemy has deep roots in many traditions, and I hold a lot of respect for that. I'm not trying to explain or teach those traditions. I'm just sharing how that spirit of transformation has shaped my life. How pain, love, survival, and time slowly turned me toward a deeper awareness of my wholeness.

And then there's Ruth. You've met her by now. My guide dog, companion, and inner voice. Ruth is alive in me not because I have a disorder, but because I am a dynamic living being. Alive. Ruth isn't a symptom. She's a truth. One of many voices in my full, layered, creative inner world. I don't have Dissociative Identity Disorder, and I hold deep care for those who do. For me, inner multiplicity isn't a diagnosis. It's a way of listening. It's how I stay in a participatory relationship with the different parts of me, and with the world inside and around me.

This is a memoir. Personal. Not prescriptive. If something stirred in you while reading, then we've already met. Somewhere deep on the inside.

Thanks for meeting me here,

Jen (and Ruth)

How Our House Became A Home

Foundation
To Mama, whose love is messy, missing, miraculous, and mine.

To Dad, who tried.

To Big Brother, who carried more than his share and still held space for me to be a baby sister.

To Lamar, the blue-eyed angel who loved and believed in me unconditionally, as I did him.

Framing
To my Iris, the one who holds our frame steady. You never flinched at the mess, just helped me through it. I choose you, again and again, every beam, every breath, every room in this home we've made together.

To Frannie, the guru who made me a mom with those bright, beautiful galaxies in her eyes.

To Ruth, my co-narrator, inner compass, and unflinching witness. The one who never stopped barking at the truth. The one who never left my side, even when I did.

Support Beams

To the ones who showed up with hammers, donations, quiet presence, and loud generosity. To every friend, neighbor, repair person, janitor, doctor, nurse, stranger, volunteer, and soul who lifted us when the load got too heavy for us to carry alone. You live in these walls. You're the warmth inside. You are part of this house, forever.

Floorboards

To my friends who believed in me, loved me through every hard part. The ones who kept watch and reeled me back in when I forgot what I was doing.

Walls

To my animal kinfolk, the furred, feathered, and scaled wild ones who've kept me alive more times than I can count.

Roof

To our Earth home that feeds, holds, teaches, and loves us, even when we forget how to reciprocate the care.

Hallways, Doors & Rooms

To every part of me that warned, worked, wrote, worried, and waited for this book to arrive, I'm so proud of what we did, together.

All my love. All my gratitude.

About The Author

Jen Peer Rich, PhD is an author, artist, and autoethnographer whose work explores healing, multiplicity, and the spiritual architecture of selves. Her debut memoir, The Alchemy of Being a House, is the first in The Circle of Selves Trilogy, a series of intimate, genre-defying books tracing the nonlinear path of trauma integration and homecoming.

With a background in ecological philosophy and decades of lived experience as a disabled, queer caregiver, Jen brings a rare blend of insight, humor, and radical compassion to her storytelling. She writes in collaboration with her many inner selves-including Ruth, a loyal inner watchdog who speaks in barked wisdom. She lives in Florida beside a lake with her beloved wife, daughter, and rescue dogs.

When she's not writing, Jen moderates conversations on conscious living, creates art and shares her healing journey with a growing community on her social media page, Jen Peer Rich is Healing.

jenpeerrich.com

Next In
The Circle of Selves Trilogy

Book Two: *Rage Was Our First Language: The Book of Baby Jenny*. This memoir is about infant fury, sacred survival, and the long return to relationship with my most innocent, innermost parts.

Before words. Before masks. Before anyone understood what she needed, there was Baby Jenny. Feral. Furious. Uncontainable. The self that was never soothed, only managed. The one who knew, even in infancy, what was and wasn't safe. In this second memoir in The Circle of Selves, we descend into our body's earliest knowing, where survival first bloomed as rage.

What happens when the traumatized baby self is finally listened to? What if the rage was never too much, just never truly welcomed or understood? What happens when that baby is given a voice to speak?

Coming Fall 2026. (*Maybe sooner, if Baby Jenny has anything to say about it!*)

Circle of Selves Press

Published by Circle of Selves Press, a home for books shaped by voice, truth, and the sacred, messy spiral of becoming. We believe every part belongs, and every voice, inner and outer, has a story worth hearing. This book is the first in a trilogy born of that vision.

Our sigil symbols tell the story:

Eye — Awareness

Arrow — Direct perception

Tree ring — Time and growth

Sprouting figure — Earth-centered, embodied becoming

Pen — How we speak truth

Dog — Loyalty to all our parts